Master · Classes

PETER ERSKINE
drum concepts and techniques

By PETER ERSKINE

Produced by John Cerullo
Art Direction by John Flannery
Edited by Rick Mattingly
Cover Photo by Darren Young

21st CENTURY MUSIC PRODUCTIONS

Distributed by Hal Leonard Publishing Corp.

THEN...

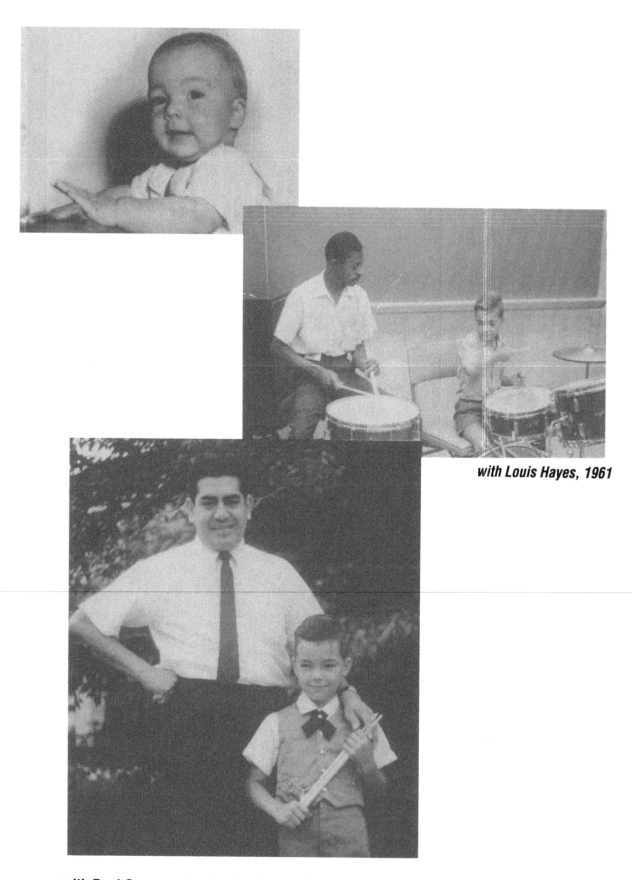

with Louis Hayes, 1961

with Paul Guerrero, instructor, Kenton Jazz Camp, Indiana

NOW...

ACKNOWLEDGEMENT

In this book, I've attempted to translate my pedagogical method into print. This methodology has been largely experiential and verbally oriented. My work in teaching and sharing whatever tips and insights I've gained over the years with younger drummers has not relied on the use of too many drumbooks; I hope, then, that this book will, by virtue of some intrinsic value, justify its own existence and find a place in the drum world.

Many thanks to: Rick Mattingly, who so expertly helped to put much of the text together; John Cerullo, who gave me the opportunity to write and present these ideas; Masamichi Asaishi of *JazzLife* Magazine; my mother and father, who originally inspired this and most of my musical ideas; Frank Baluffi, for his help with the transcriptions; Bill Ludwig III and Steven Ross & Associates, who helped provide photographs; and Mutsuko Mano, for giving me a quiet place and a computer with *WordStar* with which to work (actually, this book was written largely on the *Macintosh* computer).

To all of the above I express my gratitude and share of any credit; for any errors, I alone accept responsibility.

This book is dedicated to the memory of Shelly Manne, Collin Walcott, and Buddy Rich.

FOREWORD

To look at the recent history of American music is to look at the history of our times. Music has always captured the fire and imagination of a generation's people: Witness the Jazz Age, swing, rock and roll, folk music, The Beatles, and so on, leading up to jazz-rock, fusion, and the music that we are listening to and playing today — a music made up of pop, rhythm & blues, rock, jazz, and ethnic music influences. In other words, today's music is made up of a TOTAL SUM of the more popular styles of music that have survived the past decades.

The best, and most interesting musicians today, are those whose playing reflects an understanding of these styles — those musicians who appreciate the history of modern American Music, and have learned from it. (I freely use the term "modern American Music" to relate to the idea of this great melting pot of musical influences from around the world, realizing themselves on these shores of the Land of the Free, the Land of the Recording Industry, and the Land of the best jazz musicians in the world.) To understand a bit of history is to allow yourself to get a better idea about the future, let alone the present.

It is my opinion (as is the above) that as musicians, particularly *drummers*, grow more and more on their instrument, that sophistication inevitably leads them to an appreciation of some of the great JAZZ drumming masters. It is also my belief that, sooner or later, the aspiring professional drummer will have to play some jazz music — *convincingly*. The reverse is true for the "just jazz" drummer. In other words, drummers must be more *universal* in scope today than ever before, because the musical styles, influences, and beats have all converged.

In my own case, my musical vocabulary has been influenced by not only jazz, pop, and R&B artists, but also by the music of such composers as Edgar Varése ("Ionisation"), Igor Stravinsky ("L'Histoire du Soldat"), and Bela Bartók ("Sonata for Two Pianos and Percussion").

There's room for every kind of musical influence, but in order to take advantage of these influences, basic drumming techniques will have to be mastered to meet the challenge of today's (and tomorrow's) music.

In this book, I am going to share my drumming experiences and philosophies with you. We shall explore all of the rhythmic influences that make up my understanding of music — in other words, my drumming vocabulary and techniques. (A quick glance at the Table of Contents should give you a good idea of this book's overview.)

With WEATHER REPORT (2nd from left)

With STEPS AHEAD (2nd from left)

CONTENTS

PETER ERSKINE

Autobiography

I started playing the drums when I was three or four years old. My father fashioned a drum setup for me using an old Chinese tom-tom, a conga drum, and a sizzle cymbal (with paper clips). Dad, who was a bass player back in his college days, was just starting his career as a psychiatrist, and his office adjoined the house. As I was practicing the drums, he was analyzing people's dreams. Both he and his patients were gracious enough not to complain about my drumming. Indeed, both my mother and father, as well as my brother and two sisters, encouraged me completely.

When I had just turned seven, I met Stan Kenton at one of his week-long summer jazz band camps. Every summer thereafter I would trek off to the campus of whatever host university the camp was at and get my year's worth of jazz nourishment. During those summer camps I was lucky enough to study with drummers such as Paul Guerrero, Clem DeRosa, Charlie Perry, Dee Barton, Alan Dawson, and Ed Soph, and to be around musicians such as Oliver Nelson, Ron Carter, Jimmy Garrison, Donald Byrd, Marvin Stamm, and Johnny Richards, as well as the entire Kenton Orchestra. Thus began a relationship that culminated when I became the drummer in Stan's band at the age of eighteen.

Meanwhile, during junior high school, I studied xylophone with Billy Dorn. As high school (and football season and marching band) loomed ahead of me, I applied to, and was accepted at, the Interlochen Arts Academy, where I enjoyed playing in the symphony orchestra and the very fine jazz band there. It is an excellent school. After high school, one year of college study followed at Indiana University, with Professor George Gaber. Then I took the job with Kenton and went on the road for the next three years.

In Kenton's band I started to learn about the importance of *time-keeping*, as opposed to just playing the drums for fun and profit. Nothing is more valuable than playing day after day and night after night, receiving support, criticism, and feedback from musicians who know more than you do. I am forever grateful to Stan and the entire band.

Two years with Maynard Ferguson followed. More of the same — learning about drums and learning about life. Finally, Jaco Pastorius heard me with Maynard one night, and soon thereafter I was invited to join Weather Report. Jaco, Josef Zawinul, and Wayne Shorter are great musicians and human beings; being with them opened up all sorts of doors for me. I was with the Report for four years. I lived in Los Angeles for three of those years, and I got to play with some great musicians out there, making records with folks such as Freddie Hubbard and Joni Mitchell, doing film dates, and just playing around town.

I moved to New York City in 1982, where I played with some of my favorite musicians (guys like Michael Brecker, Mike Mainieri [Steps Ahead], Eddie Gomez, John Abercrombie, Marc Johnson, John Scofield, Don Grolnick, Will Lee, Kenny Kirkland), worked with the groups Bass Desires and Weather Update, free-lanced, composed, and taught. Recently I relocated in Southern California, where I plan to keep learning more and more about music, electronics, MIDI, production in the studio, and computers. There's plenty of room in California to raise a family, and that's just what I'm going to do.

I do love getting the chance to play, and lately there has been plenty of that!

Peter Erskine
April 1987

PETER ERSKINE

SETUP OF THE DRUMS

Let's first examine the physical setup of the drums, the physical setup of ourselves in relation to the instrument, and the hand grips of the sticks.

A Brief History

The drum setup has evolved from a relatively primitive, though ingenious, design of a side drum (or snare drum) and a bass drum (with a simple pedal mechanism to play the bass drum and simultaneously strike a small mounted cymbal on the b.d. hoop) to the addition of the early hi-hat (a/k/a the "snow-shoe," then, the "low-boy"), tom-toms, and cymbals; to today's engineer-designed hardware-laden drumkits, with electronic synthesis, digital sampling and reproduction to boot.

The good old days saw some stupendous drumsets, like Sonny Greer's magnificent percussion setup in Duke Ellington's Orchestra.

And, though for a while it seemed all too true that they weren't "making them like they used to," I think that today's drummer has the choice of finding expertly made drums, cymbals, and hardware.

While some drummers prefer having many drums and cymbals around them, others prefer what is now thought of as the more traditional setup: the four-or-five-piece setup.

It is this type of setup that we will deal with in the following pages.

THE DRUMS ARE ONE INSTRUMENT

DRUMSET = YOU

My idea is that the drumset is like your body. Your right arm has one function, your nose has a function, your ears have a function, and so on. But you are one human being, and you convey ideas or physical activity as one person. It's the same with the drumset. I don't think that you should approach it as a multiple-percussion setup; it's one instrument. There are different components to it, just as there are different notes on a piano, and there are pedals on a piano. You have to learn how to use them all together to present one idea. I'm aware of the premise of having a lead voice, which is usually the ride cymbal. I don't intend, though, to isolate it from the rest of the kit. It's important how everything works together. The drumset is, indeed, one instrument, and that's why balance is so important on the kit.

Make sure that the setup is comfortable for you.

You should not have to reach too far to strike any portion of your playing area. This is important! If your seat is so high that your feet do not reach the pedals comfortably, or your cymbals are so high or far away that you must make an effort to play them, then your setup is WRONG FOR YOU.

RELAXATION is the key to doing anything truly well, especially when it involves physical motion and activity. If your setup invites fatigue or strain, how are you going to play some really good music for any length of time? So the drums and cymbals should be positioned in front of you so that you can comfortably reach every part of the kit. (I sit rather low; I find it helps me to play the pedals with more control and strength as my legs are not too long.) I think of my drum setup as a sort of cockpit: everything is right in front of me.

Avoid drastic angles. In general, you should always avoid exaggerations — in your setup, your motion, or playing style. What I am mainly referring to here is the importance of keeping the tom-toms and cymbals relatively flat. I have, in the past, made the mistake of playing my cymbals or tom-toms at too acute an angle. Not only did this make striking them more difficult (especially with any degree of consistency, as I found myself glancing off of that instrument), but also the sound suffered. The more flat a drum or cymbal is, the easier it is to hit and get a good sound from. *Period.* (I recognize that the stick-to-cymbal attitude is a unique part of certain stylistic drumming styles, a la the early '70s Al Mouzon/Eric Gravatt high-intensity ride cymbal playing where the cymbal was positioned very high and almost vertical. Like I said, I once played that way. As I've gotten older, I've discovered it's easier, and it sounds better, to play the other way. And it can still get intense — even more so, in fact.)

It's important to remember: **Your setup has to allow you to play in a relaxed manner!**

1. Shoulders down, arms by your sides.

2. Appropriate heights all the way around.

3. Don't fight your equipment. MAKE SURE
   IT IS IN GOOD WORKING CONDITION!

(I'm amazed at how some drummers' equipment has rattles, or the heads are too loose or too tight, or the drums are completely out of whack — it just makes no sense. If you play an instrument, you have to maintain it. That's a priority. It's a privilege to have a good instrument to play on. Don't treat an instrument poorly.)

The Sticks

Find the right drumsticks for YOU. Just like Goldilocks and the Three Bears, you should find them to be not too heavy, not too light, but "just right" (AAAHHHHH). Your playing situation will be a determining factor up to a point. Vic Firth once wisely said, "Where does it say that you have to settle on just one stick? Timpanists certainly don't. For lighter stuff they use a lighter stick." So why try to play lightly with a big drumstick? Use a lighter stick. If you have to play heavier, use a heavy stick. Sax players do something like that when they change mouthpieces for different applications. Guitarists use different gauge strings, and even different guitars. So the right stick choice is important.

For general use I play with the Vic Firth *7A* hickory sticks; for lighter work, I use the maple *SD 4*. For the truest cymbal sound, I prefer a wood-tipped stick.

Vic Firth has now come out with the Peter Erskine Signature model drumstick, which is beautifully balanced, with a light tip. I use it for all of my jazz work.

The Grip

Right Hand

Make sure that your grip is firm, but relaxed. For playing on the ride cymbal, my thumb is on top of the stick.

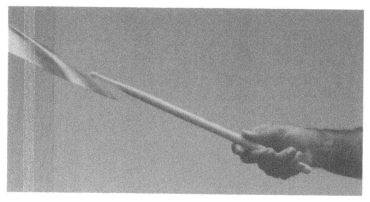

This, as opposed to the traditional snare drum grip

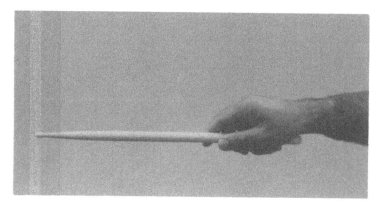

makes more sense for me for playing on the ride cymbal, because it seems to form a straighter line from my shoulder to the tip of the stick (in other words, there is no twisting of the arm). Also, I can accomplish a loose, relaxed yet powerful snapping motion.

Left Hand

I employ both the "traditional" and the "matched" grip when I play. Since the traditional grip was the first technique that I learned (when I was learning to play jazz), that is the grip I use when I'm in a jazz situation. For louder contexts, such as strong backbeats, I will play matched grip, sometimes turning the stick around and using the butt end. This is nothing new; Gene Krupa used to do it, too.

Whichever grip you use, be sure to strive for evenness and consistency in whatever you play.

Both Hands

I get a consistent rebound of close to one inch off of whatever part of the drumkit I'm playing on — snare drum, tom-tom, hi-hat, or ride cymbal. This ensures that the stick is in the area where it's going to be doing its business. Each stroke originates from the same place: this ensures consistency. Don't originate your strokes from up in the air; that's where a good margin for error can creep in. You *can* bring the stick back for more power, but always start from the same place. This will keep your playing motion and activity FOCUSED.

A good drum stroke involves a "**snap**," that is, hitting the drum with velocity (speed) and quickly lifting the stick off of the head. This can be done at any dynamic level.

I hold the sticks pretty close to the butt ends. I like to do this because of the leverage factor. I also hold the sticks in a very relaxed manner; this helps with the overall concept of relaxation, and is also an important part of letting the stick absorb as much of the impact shock as possible. If you are holding the sticks tightly and in a brittle fashion, and you hit a drum or cymbal very hard, something has got to give; it may, unfortunately, be your stick, your cymbal, or part of YOU.

Remember:

1. Hold the sticks firm but loose.

2. All drumming utilizes a combination of finger, wrist, and arm usage.

3. It is essential that the drummer always play *relaxed*, and get the most out of his or her body potential.

RIDE CYMBAL
CONCEPT & TECHNIQUE

Jazz music, arguably America's greatest artistic contribution to the world, has a wonderful history, one that goes back well beyond the halcyon days of Storyville (in New Orleans). It will benefit *all* musicians to acquaint themselves with early jazz and Afro-American musics. I would like to focus this chapter, however, on the music and drumming style that comes directly from "bebop" (which evolved from "swing"), for I feel this style is the *cornerstone* to successful *modern* drumming.

It is my sincere belief that the better a drummer's understanding of and ability to play good time is, the better a musician that drummer is going to get the chance to be. Duke Ellington said, "It don't mean a thing if it ain't got that swing." *All* music has to swing — especially jazz! The drummer's ride cymbal plays a key part in this prerequisite.

Ride Cymbal Concept

The **quarter-note pulse** is the primary rhythmic factor in contemporary music, whether it be jazz, rock, funk, or pop music. The **eighth** and **sixteenth** notes, or **subdivisions** of the bar, determine the **feel** of the music (i.e., "swung" eighth notes as compared to "straight" eighth notes). In jazz, the eighth notes are generally swung. Two swung eighth notes resemble the first and third beats of an eighth-note triplet.

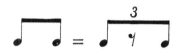

Traditionally, the jazz cymbal pattern has been notated:

It's not played quite that way, however. The ride-cymbal pattern is more like this:

If a classically minded musicologist were to attempt to notate the rhythm of jazz, it might look like this!

Written notation is only an approximation of the actual placement of the swung eighth note. However, for our purposes, I shall notate the ride-cymbal pattern as follows:

A ride-cymbal pattern may be phrased any way that the drummer "hears" it — the bottom line in all of this is that it has to sound good — but **consistency** and **clarity** are of the utmost importance. The other musicians that you are playing with, as well as your audience, must be able to clearly hear and feel the pulse of the time and your subdivisions.

As a starting point, do *not* accent the beats 2 and 4 on the ride cymbal. By way of example, think of a walking 4/4 bass line:

The bass does not accent on 2, 4, or any one beat of the bar. Each quarter-note pulse is as important as the next; driving and moving forward. This applies to any tempo of 4/4.

The ride cymbal should be thought of in the same context as the bass:

Accenting the beats 2 and 4 usually results in the drummer physically (and thus, sonically) breaking up the bar of 4/4 into two halves. And then, instead of a *bona fide* quarter-note pulse, we hear instead a three-note phrase:

This three-note phrase can negatively manifest itself when the drummer attempts to "dance" with, or change up, the cymbal beat from the basic:

such as:

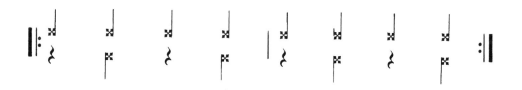

The detrimental aspect of this is that the clarity of the quarter-note pulse is gone — not only to the other musicians and listeners, but internally (for the drummer) as well. My experience has shown me that, by developing the inner sense of time with full consideration of the quarter-note pulse (coordinated with the physical act of playing the ride cymbal), the drummer then builds and strengthens his or her understanding and feel for the **motion** of music.

In other words, Art Blakey has made a lot of great music while accenting the beats 2 and 4 on the ride cymbal; Elvin Jones swings harder than anybody, and he's accenting the "and" of 2 and 4. Both of these drumming masters play it the way they hear it, but at the same time, these gentlemen are fully conscious of the role of the quarter-note pulse.

It is important to know that music is **linear**. From music's very beginning, its sound has moved in a linear, **horizontal** fashion. I'm talking left-to-right, here-to-there; the beat is *going* someplace! Think of time playing (i.e., the ride cymbal) as not only the motor, but also the golden thread that weaves through and connects the music.

Practice playing a "driving" quarter-note pulse on the ride cymbal, with the hi-hat playing on beats 2 and 4.

Remember: You get out of your instrument what you put into it. Play with snap and "electricity," in other words, **energy**, without exaggerating your motions or the sound.

Note: We all march to the beat of a slightly different drummer in terms of our internal clock, or where we comfortably like to play tempo-wise. Be able to play different grooves at **all** tempos. This is important!

     Remember:

     1. Consistent stick rebound.

     2. Don't play on "top" of the cymbal.
        Get some weight and the meat
        of your arm in there. Think of gravity.

     3. Keep it light.

     4. Play relaxed.

Now let's add the swung eighth-note syncopation to the quarter note. How you phrase the swung eighth note is your drumming signature.

Adding the swung eighth notes to the quarter notes will change the arm motion slightly. Think of the swung eighth note as a pickup to the next quarter note, in that the downward arm motion for the quarter notes on beats 1 and 3 is part of the same downward arm motion for the swung offbeat eighth note. Don't move so much of the entire arm to play the syncopation. Use more of the wrist and fingers. The weight and velocity of the quarter-note pulse will thus not be affected. Keep in mind the consistency of rebound and sound.

Play the following exercise: the ride cymbal pattern with hi-hat on 2 and 4 at a slow to moderate tempo, e.g. mm = 80 and work it up to mm = 176.

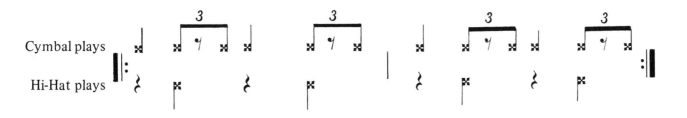

Try to keep the eighth notes swung even at the faster tempos. It is possible to play the eighth notes in a more "straight" up and down fashion, a la Tony Williams with the Miles Davis band in the '60s, at a variety of tempos. Certainly, faster tempos invite the straight eighth-note approach. Be able to play both ways.

(I will address FAST and SLOW tempos more thoroughly a little bit later.)

Expanding the sound possibilities of the ride cymbal is simple. The typical bebop ride-cymbal pattern is played on the ride area part of the cymbal. Try playing closer to the bell, or on the bell. You can play on the bell of the cymbal to approximate a cowbell sound for Latin beats, and also play quarter, eighth, or half-note beats on the bell to cut through the high volume of a band — a very driving sound.

You can also play ("dancing" with the stick) around and on the bell in a jazz framework; it's very modern sounding (I used it a lot with Weather Report. Josef Zawinul showed it to me. I worked on it, developed it, and he loved it).

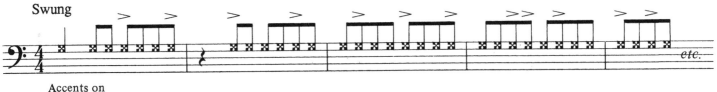

Accents on
Bell of Cymbal

Playing the cymbal with the butt end of the drum stick will result in a loud and very strong cymbal beat (best played near the bell). Another textural effect on the ride cymbal is achieved by playing on the edge, with the shank of the stick. This accent can be played in unison (together) with a snare or bass drum beat.

Of course, crash cymbal playing involves striking the cymbal's edge in a sweeping motion. Avoid striking straight down on a cymbal, as this, repeatedly done, could cause cracking.

N.B. Allow your cymbals to breathe! **DO NOT** clamp down and choke a cymbal on its stand. A cymbal's truest sound comes from its ability to vibrate freely. You can control a cymbal's dynamic response by how you play it. This advice is not just musical. You can risk cracking a cymbal if it cannot vibrate freely. Cymbals sound so good — let them sing!

"There are no limits out there . . . if you can conceive of it (in your mind),
you can produce it on your instrument. With work."
— Professor Jiggs Whigham
    Musikhochschule
    Köln, West Germany

To listen is to receive the best instruction.

Listen to as many recordings as you can of the great drummers. Any opportunity that you have to hear good music live, DO IT. You not only gain inspiration and learn a lot, but you also support the art form.

To play is to realize self expression.

No single musician invented jazz. Jazz is a music that is alive with tradition, with its eye, heart, and mind aimed at tomorrow (in other words, NOW! Now means improvised, spontaneous, and instinctive composition vis-a-vis playing).

Why try to invent something that Tony Williams played, when he has already played it? Take advantage of the history of music, learn from it, and then add to it.There is no sense in trying to figure it all out from scratch without some help from the people who do it best.

LISTEN!

Acquire a musical VOCABULARY.

After you've done some listening, then you will have a sound inside of your head. After you've got a sound inside of your head, you will have the musical urge to play it on your instrument. If it's jazz, then you will have an idea of where to place the swung eighth note. I recommend listening to the ride cymbal playing of Philly Joe Jones, Art Blakey, Max Roach, Roy Haynes, Elvin Jones, et al, for a better idea of what I'm talking about.

*"What makes a jazz drummer is his ability to take any group, whether it's a small group or a big band, and hold those cats together and get something swinging, whatever tempo: up, down, medium. **The function of a jazz drummer is to instill in the other players a force which, in turn, makes the jazz players play better."***

— Buddy Rich, revealing his affinity for the philosophy of drumming
as expounded by Jo Jones in a *down beat* magazine interview.

INDEPENDENCE

"Give me liberty, or give me Jim Chapin's phone number!"

— a not too well-known drummer

Drumming is one of the few things in this world that requires so much coordination and independence of the four extremeties. I imagine that piloting a helicopter comes the closest to the demands of playing a drumset. That being said, I personally feel that independence is, in itself, no big deal. Certainly it is necessary to have! But, as I like to point out at clinics or any gathering of drummers, if you can rub your belly and pat your head at the same time, then change hands doing it, you can tackle independence on the drumset, which involves getting the four limbs to interrelate and work together in a smooth, coordinated manner. Any drummer is capable of developing a high degree of independence; all that it takes is practice.

It is important to stress, however, that no amount of independence or "chops" is any good if the drummer is not swinging! This is not something to be taken for granted. The ride cymbal must be "happening," strong and swinging, *consistently!* Discipline and technique give you the means to say something on your instrument, but these things must be coupled with musical intelligence and aesthetic sensibility.

The ideal state of independence means, for me, that **you** are in control; if you hear a rhythmical, or other musical elemental idea inside of your head, you can play it on the drums — without being limited by one of your hands or feet dictating **what** should go **where**. We all have idiosyncracies, like when your right hand does one thing, the left responds in kind — dependent on habits that you've built up over months and years. More often than not, you won't be aware of these idiosyncratic liabilities. Where this can really show up, and be damaging, is when you are playing the ride cymbal (4/4 jazz pattern) — which is most of the time (in jazz) — and when the left hand goes to play something, simple or complex, the ride cymbal beat changes up — unintentionally. It's the same with the left and right feet. I was a victim of (and a culprit to) this situation, and only until the first couple of professional recordings that I had made (with Stan Kenton) came out did I become aware of it.

The following **Basic Independence Exercises** have proven, in my experience, to be both a terrific training system for 4/4 jazz time-keeping and a sure-fire litmus test of a drummer's independence. **The simplicity of these exercises is their chief asset.** These basic rhythms make up the core of drumming's vocabulary; these rhythms are, simply, either on or off the beat. The fancy stuff can come later. **Be sure that you can play all of the following, without changing up the actual rhythm, feel, or intensity of the ride cymbal!**

Remember:

1. Start with just the ride cymbal and hi-hat. Begin at a comfortable tempo.

2. The swung, offbeat eighth note falls in the same place as the last note of the eighth-note triplet; in other words, it coincides with the ride-cymbal pattern.

3. Dynamics! The relative dynamics of the snare drum to the ride cymbal to the bass drum to the hi-hat, etc., is fundamentally and musically important!

4. Be able to play these and *swing* at all tempos, slow to fast.

BASIC INDEPENDENCE EXERCISES

Snare Drum

In this book, always remember the following:

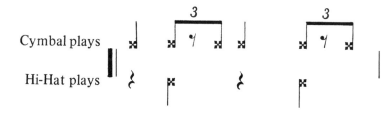

Cymbal plays

Hi-Hat plays

Snare Drum: Play relaxed, balanced with the ride cymbal, and take note of how much motion you are applying to the playing. In other words, use the appropriate amount of arm (in this case, none) wrist and finger movement to exercise these rhythms on the snare drum.

The snare drum is generally struck near the center of the head, as are the tom-toms. Try hitting the drumhead closer to the edge, and listen to the difference. This tonal difference can be effective. Use your ears and imagination.

A **rim shot** is played one of three ways:

1) playing the stick across the head and rim (see illustration).

2) hitting the drum head and rim at the same time with the stick.
   This is the most common method for obtaining a strong **backbeat**.

3) laying the left hand stick across the head and rim, and hitting with the other stick.

The first method is associated with jazz drumming, like that of Philly Joe Jones, or with samba and bossa nova styles, and so on. Rim shots (second method) can be played on tom-toms as well.

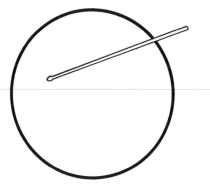

Find the "sweet spot" of the stick. (Listen to the difference between rebounding the stick off the rim about one inch, and just letting the stick sit on the rim. I always rebound.)

I rest the last three fingers of my left hand on the snare drum head ("pinkie" first).

Snare Drum

J

K

L

M

N

O

P

Q

R

S

T

U

V Shuffle - like

W Swung or

X "Straight"

Y

Z

Bass Drum

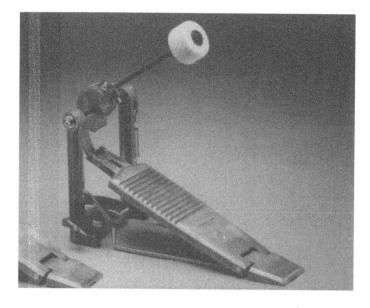

My bass drum pedal technique involves playing with the heel down, or flat on the pedal board, for soft to medium-loud passages where not too much speed is involved. (When your feet are flat on the pedals, you have better balance and control.) For louder playing, or multiple-note figures, I go up onto the ball, or "toe," of my foot on the pedal. playing further back on the pedal board. In the course of playing those multiple notes, my foot will move forward along the pedal board.

For loud volume, I use more of my leg; i.e., I play on the ball of my foot and take advantage of the weight of my leg. Again, leverage, as well as bringing the beater back for a full, strong stroke, is a factor. Be aware of the two different tones that you will get from a bass drum by (1) letting the beater ball come off the head after striking, or (2) leaving the beater ball against the head after striking it. There is a definite sound difference, *especially* when playing a double-headed bass drum.

I find that seat height can also be an important factor in how you play the bass drum. I, myself, sit rather low at the kit.

I use the Yamaha *FP-710* pedal. It's their lighter model, and it's terrific. I simply took it out of the box and began playing on it. I keep the tension relatively loose.

Conception

In early swing music, the drummer played the bass drum on all four beats of the bar (sometimes quite predominantly). With the advent of bebop, the bass drum began to be used more for accents and highly syncopated "kicks" — that is to say, much freer. Today, how you wish to use the bass drum is up to you. Playing sofly on all four beats adds a nice bottom to the sound. A modern drummer must be familiar with this way of playing, as well as with the freer style.

Now let's play these same types of basic rhythms on the bass drum while playing the ride cymbal and hi-hat as before.

Remember, be aware of relative dynamics. In other words, don't overpower the ride cymbal with the bass drum.

Bass Drum

A

J

K

L

M

N

O

P

Q

Snare and Bass Drum Combinations

Now we combine some of the basic rhythms from the previous snare and bass drum exercises. (Same rules for the Ride Cymbal and Hi-Hat).

Snare and Bass Drum

The Hemiola

A grouping of accents within one meter that resembles another meter (for example, two against three,

See exercises F and G, Snare and Bass Drum Combinations. While the meter is clearly in four, the accents are every three beats (eighth notes). If you have ever listened to Elvin Jones you have heard one example of this.

Note: the right hand is playing 4/4, the left hand and bass drum are playing 3/4 time (in duple rhythm).

Remember: The last note of an eighth-note triplet lands in the same place as the swung offbeat eighth note. Both will fit in with the ride-cymbal pattern.

"In point of fact, Elvin, with his former associates John Coltrane and McCoy Tyner, is responsible for the development of an entirely new way of sensing jazz rhythm — a way now so familiar to us that it has almost come to be taken for granted. In much the same fashion as did Max Roach and Kenny Clarke in the forties, during the sixties Elvin has literally revolutionized jazz drumming through his use of polyrhythmic accents in the left hand (and high-hat cymbal). Today, thanks to him, we think nothing of listening to a piece that appears at one and the same time to be in quadruple and triple meter — that is, in both four and three. But there was a time when this was by no means the case. It remained for Elvin to show us that it was possible to juxtapose a steady stream of triplet figures in the left hand against a basic quarter-note beat in the right, while making the entire operation swing with a well-nigh irresistible force."

— Frank Kofsky, quoted by Joachim-Ernst Berendt,
"Jazz: A Photo History," Schirmer Books, 1979

" . . . it's not the licks that are important. It's the atmosphere of spontaneity, and the things that are playing off of each other that cause other things to happen.

"You must first spend a long time doing time doing everything that the great drummers do. Then you can understand what it means. I've found that not only do you learn how to play something, but you also learn why it was played. That's the value of playing like someone. You can't just learn a lick. You've got to learn where it came from, what caused the drummer to play that way, and a number of things. Drumming is like an evolutionary pattern.

"What I play is a reaction to what is going on around me."
— Tony Williams, *Modern Drummer,* June 1984

Discipline yourself to keep the ride cymbal "happening" while playing all manner of rhythms on the rest of the kit; this will pay off in confident time-keeping that swings. As a piano player "comps" (short for ac**comp**animent), so does the drummer; jazz is an ever changing, spontaneous dialogue between musicians — *improvisation*. These exercises are good stepping stones toward the drummer's mastery of the language. Remember — use your ears, too!

Hi-Hat and Ride Cymbal Combination

Play ride   as before.

Hi-Hat
A

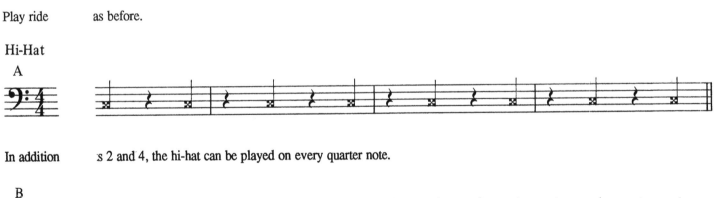

In addition   s 2 and 4, the hi-hat can be played on every quarter note.

B

For snare drum/hi-hat interplay, practice playing the hi-hat on the off beats (& of 1, & of 2, etc.)

C

Snare/Hi-hat combinations

Play ride cymbal as before.

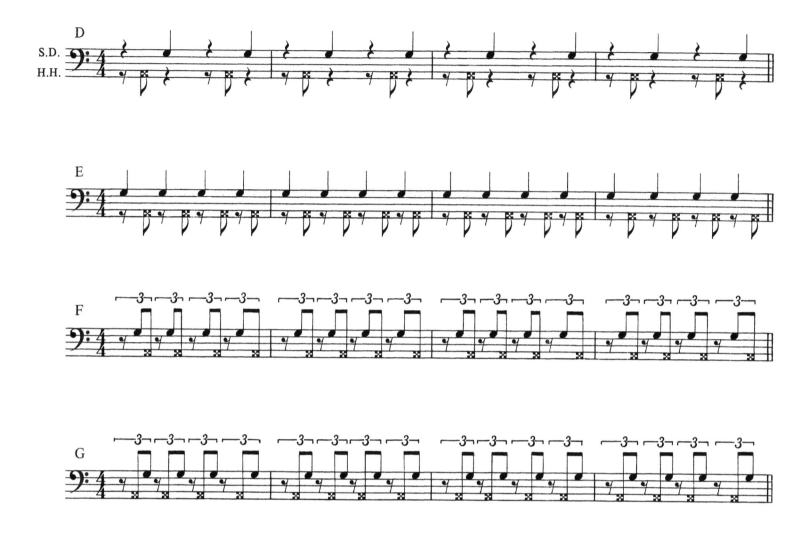

Ride cymbal/Hi-hat combinations

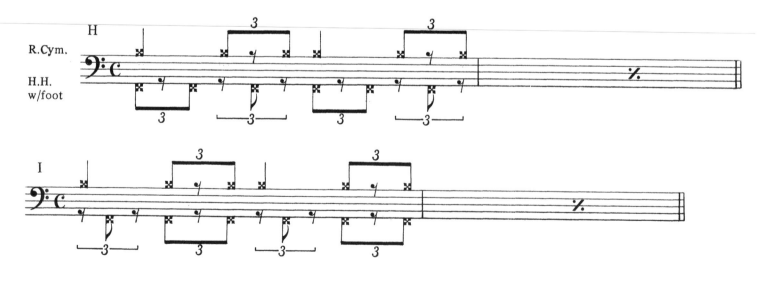

Ride Cymbal/Snare/Hi-hat combinations

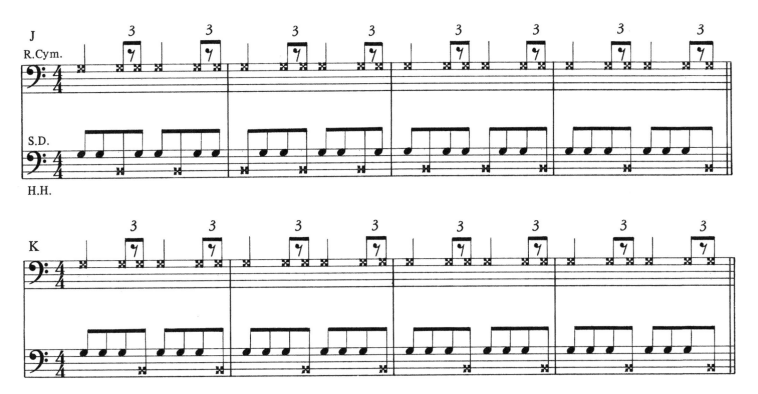

Now let's change up the ride cymbal pattern slightly. The following rhythm is actually a 3/4 ride-cymbal pattern played within a 4/4 context. Thus, we explore bar-line phrasing and polyrhythms. The importance of the quarter note's clarity, integrity, and pulse becomes clear (as well as that of the eighth note's).

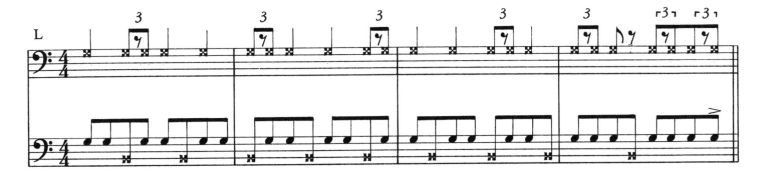

The right hand is playing 3/4 rhythmic feel, etc. Now see exercises F and G, Snare and Bass Drum Combinations again. Anything is possible, as long as it swings.

Which brings me to a most important point: THE EXTENSION OF THE BASICS OF YOUR TIME KEEPING MANIFESTS ITSELF THUSLY: THE UNDERLYING STRENGTH SUPPORTS ANY SYNCOPATION ON TOP — SIMPLE OR COMPLEX.

And by this I mean not only the underlying strength of an obvious rhythm or pattern, but the strength that is **in** you, the musician. Your experience, knowledge, and confidence will support your imagination.

Hi-Hat Control—Foot Exercises (No Stick)

You can change the texture of the hi-hat sound. One way is, instead of closing the hi-hat cymbals tightly against each other, play them with a stick while varying the amount of space and tension between the top and bottom cymbals. Or, with your left foot alone, get a rhythmic "swoosh" sound by bringing the hi-hat cymbals together and then popping them apart. This is done by lifting the toe quickly from the pedal board. Practice will bring complete control over the hi-hat pedal. The cymbals are alive now!

SLOW AND FAST TEMPOS

Slow Tempos

Most drummers are only concerned with learning to play fast tempos, but in fact, slow tempos are just as difficult. The problem, of course, is not from the point of view of technique, or chops if you will. With slow tempos, concentration is the name of the game, and it's also a matter of trusting yourself enough to know that simple timekeeping will work the best. This is the only way that I've found to play slow tempos: by NOT FILLING UP ALL THE SPACES BETWEEN THE BEATS. Every note that you play must count for something. Every time you play a note on the drumset, you are sending it out into space. It can be compared to putting "English" on a cue ball: The kind of velocity you put on the beat and the quality of the space between each beat determine the motion of the music. Medium tempos are easy because we're comfortable with the amount of space in between beats. But with slow tempos, there is a lot of space (relatively speaking) between the beats. So you have to concentrate and really zero in on the pulse.

Phrasing

There are two ways to phrase the slow ride-cymbal pattern. One is in the relaxed triplet sense:

The other is through quasi double time: The dotted eighth/sixteenth, or double dotted eighth/thirty-second.

This could be notated as the following:

This notation implies a double-time feel.

You have to be careful with the quasi double-time type of interpretation. The subliminal undercurrent of whatever subdivision you're thinking of will come out in your playing whether you explicitly play it or not. So if you don't mean to imply double time, then you shouldn't play it. In other words, if the song has a relaxed, swung eighth note, triplet-feeling kind of groove, suddenly going into double time will not fit the pulse. The slow triplet (or swung eighth note) groove is more fitting, and it's more relaxed; it swings better. So be aware of the nature of the groove for each tune and play accordingly.

Fast Tempos

As the tempos become faster, the amount of space between the beats becomes less and less. As a result, in the very fast tempos, you don't have as much time to swing the eighth notes. The ride-cymbal pattern begins to sound like a quarter note and two straight eighth notes.

Note: Tony Williams often played this rhythm with Miles Davis at medium to fast tempos, i.e., "Madness," from *Nefertitti*.

As I go up the tempo scale, I personally like to keep the eighth notes swung a little further up on the scale than a lot of drummers do. Of course, it depends on the style of music. If you want to play a straight-eighth-note pattern a la the Tony Williams example, then that kind of groove works well not only at very fast tempos, but at moderately fast and medium ones, too.

I approach fast tempos by thinking slow. If I try to concentrate on each note, I'm stuck right there. So instead of getting wrapped up in every little beat, I try to see the big picture: the downbeats, or even two- or four-bar phrases. I take advantage of the multi-levels of the time movement. If I'm focusing on the individual beats, I'm moving in small, fast steps. I prefer to move in big, slower steps. I'm still playing all of the fast stuff, but by looking far enough ahead, I don't miss the curves. So it all has to do with looking at music and rhythm as a whole. It's not the little beats; it's the phrases and statements, all within the realm of timekeeping.

Even though I'm not thinking about every little note, I *am* articulating every pulse on the ride cymbal — particularly the quarter-note pulse. There is a certain amount of controlled bounce that comes into play on fast tempos, but I'm not just slapping the stick down on 2 and 4, and hoping that the bounce will carry me through to the next 2 or 4. That doesn't work. You still have to work the pulse while being aware of the big picture.

Another important thing to remember when playing fast tempos is to PLAY RELAXED. This not only pertains to the right hand, but also to getting the left-hand interplay happening. Many drummers get all tensed up and make too big a production out of playing fast; they put too much effort into it. You have to be relaxed when you play music, no matter what the tempo. Also, you can play faster when you don't worry about playing fast. That sounds like a paradox, but it's true! Not being bound by tension and anxiety frees you up to play your fastest because you are as relaxed as if you were playing a moderate tempo. Relaxation also comes from being prepared: practicing and having the equipment there, so that you feel in a state of readiness. You don't have to be all flexed up. You can play almost any tempo with confidence; just get the tempo set in your mind, give yourself an upbeat to get started, and wail!

When I'm playing fast, particularly if it's not extremely loud or doesn't require a lot of muscle power, I keep my feet flat on the pedals for the best balance and control. I like to fly when I have to play fast; I try to stay light on my feet, dance with the music, and see the big picture. I give myself rhythmic signposts along the way, such as strong accents that determine the form of a particular phrase. Just remember that you can't squeeze as much into a fast tempo as you can with a medium tempo. And by the same token, even though you can squeeze a whole lot into a slow tempo, you will not necessarily want to and probably shouldn't.

Concentration, relaxation, and discretion are three very important elements. They must be combined with enough practice so that you have the ability to play any tempo that you're bound to be confronted with in your particular musical environment. For some professionals, that environment can be just about anything.

STRAIGHT(ER) EIGHTH-NOTE RHYTHMS — ACCENTS AND VARIATIONS

The Role of Accents, and Accents Within A Phrase

Note: The progression through the following beats and examples reveals the genesis and evolution of my own playing style. You are encouraged to look at it only as an example and possible starting point.

So far, we've discussed the quarter-note pulse and its fundamental importance in mainstream music, and we've discussed the subdivisions of that quarter-note pulse. In the case of eighth-note subdivisions, the eighth notes can be either straight or swung. We've talked about the triplet feel in relation to the swung eighth notes, but I don't think that you should subdivide the eighth notes into triplet groupings, singing the silent second note of the triplet.

I think that you can learn to internalize the swung eighth-note rhythm, because that is, in itself, a bona fide subdivision.

Now, as far as accents go, let's consider the following: Every American (and Westerns fan) knows this beat.

There are four quarter notes with the accent on the first beat (**downbeat**) of the 4/4 bar. We can make a variation of that by moving the accent to the second beat.

That's an example of an **upbeat**, and while it is interesting, that particular rhythm doesn't really do much for you as a listener or a drummer. But this next example is something that everyone around the world can recognize: It's a strong **backbeat**.

Continuing along these variation lines, we follow with this:

Let's now think in the more open terms of a two-bar phrase. By more open, I mean that there is more room for the accent to be played and digested.

The same idea can be applied to eighth notes. First, the one-bar phrase:

Now, the two-bar phrase:

Some of these eighth-note examples are catching the quarter-note accents that we've already examined, but there are also those extra, in-between ones, still within the two-bar realm. Breaking that down into sixteenth notes

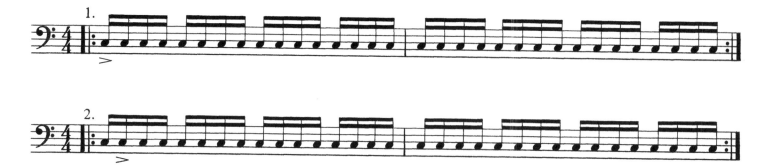

you can see very readily the infinite possibilities. These are just one-beat accents within the space of two bars; we first started with quarter notes, then eighth notes, and then sixteenth notes. Of course, extra accents can be included. This opens up the entire **universe** of rhythmic possibilities. That universe can be looked at in one of two ways: chaotic, as certain scientists perceive our universe, or closer to Einstein's hope that God did not play dice with the universe and that there is some order in it.

Practical applications of the previous examples include:

1. Time-keeping exercises, e.g., a simple, straight eighth-note beat that incorporates the accented point in the bar, with either a simple fill leading up to it, or no fill at all.

2. Playing on a closed hi-hat, experiment with the different accents while the bass drum plays on beats 1 and 3, or 2 and 4, or beats 1, 2, 3, and 4. Add the snare drum to this, first starting with a simple backbeat, and then try syncopating the snare (e.g., the fourth sixteenth of the first beat). Differently accented sixteenth notes on the hi-hat help to give flow to the beat and the music, and it is quite characteristic of my playing style.

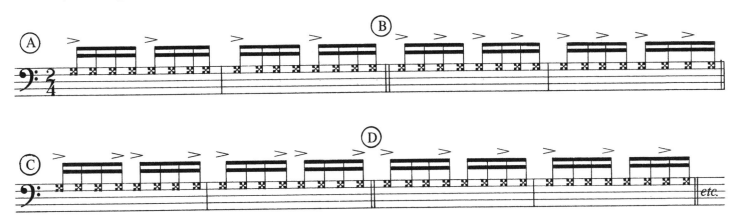

(Bob Moses treats this subject very successfully and in quite some depth in his book *Drum Wisdom*, published by Modern Drummer Publications. See the chapters dealing with the 8/8 concept, the eight points, etc.)

Back to perceptions of the universe and two-bar phrases. I like to believe that most anything goes. However, successful art and music need some structure and discipline. Along those lines then, we have to consider where we place those accents. Most of the time, the determining factor will come instinctively, just by virtue of what we've learned — in other words, the vocabulary that we've acquired. It's not so much in the form of licks. Rather, you'll hear something in the musical context that you're playing in that will trigger something in your memory and inspire you to respond to it in a certain way. This can be spontaneously, as in an improvised setting, or in creating a groove, where you should observe the following: **LISTEN TO THE BASS PLAYER; HIS PATTERN WILL GUIDE YOUR HANDS AND FEET AS TO WHAT TO PLAY.**

Because putting an accent in one place will imply a completely different feel than if you put it in another place, it's easy to see that (1) accents carry a lot of weight, and (2) they are the key to the deeper rhythmic understanding and interpretation that a musician is taking with the music.

Accents don't just come out of the blue; they generally are attached to the drummer's understanding of the levels of time that are moving by. Levels of time are an apparent and evident concept by virtue of the illustrations that we've just gone through. Within a two-bar phrase, looking at the different placements of accents — whether within quarters, eighth notes, or sixteenths — obvious different feels come about. This is the way music is.

MUSIC IS NOT ONE DIMENSIONAL. It's three dimensional, if not four dimensional. (Perhaps it is four dimensional. I think it is, actually . . . or is that the **fifth** dimension? I'm not sure.)

What I have been attempting to talk about are accents and the grouping of accents, and how the grouping of accents represents the ebb and flow in rhythmic motion.

The Layers Of Time

I can best illustrate the different levels of time as a simple conceptual idea:

The bass drum plays four quarter notes.

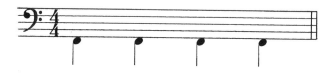

The snare drum plays a backbeat on 2 and 4.

There are two levels of pulse, both constant, and both doing their own thing — both certainly related to each other.

The hi-hat could be playing eighth notes

or it could be playing quarter notes

or offbeat eighth notes.

That's a different feel because of the upbeat.

Or sixteenth notes.

Just by changing the hi-hat, there are three or four different levels of time feeling from the same basic bass drum and snare (backbeat) idea. Those different hi-hat interpretations reveal how I'm hearing the flow and motion of this beat and of this music: Is it tight? Is it open? Is there a subtle double-time undercurrent? This is only one way of playing different levels of time. Again, the possibilities are endless.

I think that the key to any successful rhythm or beat (for starters) is **simplicity.** Now, if you listen to a successsful pop record (from any point in history), you'll discover that the drumbeat or drum part is relatively simple. "Pop" equals "popular," which usually means that you hear it whether you want to or not. But this is a good beginning to understand the concept of a simple beat, and to that you can add accent variations or whatever.

The Density Factor

Consider (1) textural density and (2) density of ideas. Drummers tend to be guilty of playing too much where they shouldn't. Don't fill up all of the spaces, and don't play a bunch of complicated things where something simple would do. There are times when eighth notes will take you a lot further than sixteenth notes. If you cloud the sound up by playing fast, it can sound like nothing's happening. But you can build excitement with fewer notes — a couple of well-chosen eighth notes here and there. Lately I have been the happiest when I have managed to just play something simple when the music called for that. Subtlety and understatement — less is more.

The bottom line for any beat is that it has to feel good, and it should make people want to dance. When something grooves, the drummer makes it sound easy. If the drummer sounds like he's breaking his neck, that's no groove.

On to a collection (or evolution) of straight eighth-note beats. *(The hi-hat can also play sixteenth and quarter notes, as we examined before.)*

"Make It Funky!"
—James Brown

BEATS

An Evolution of Rock/Funk Beats

Legend

Hi-Hat or Cymbal

Snare Drum • Rim Click ⊠ Ghost Note (•)

Bass Drum

As I continue playing and learning about music, I find that the simple beats remain the most effective, and provide the best base from which to build. So when playing a piece of music for the first time, start out with a pure, simple beat, and embellish (or subtract!) from that. (Listen to: Rick Marotta, Russ Kunkel, Al Jackson, Bernard Purdie, Jeff Porcaro, Steve Gadd, and Chris Parker, or any Motown and James Brown records.)

In the following examples, the bass drum is first used to play simple parts. Gradually the bass drum's parts become more complex, resulting in some complicated beats. In these more complicated beats, the bass drum serves more as a lead voice. In order to develop this lead voice concept, begin with a simple bass drum part that provides a strong foundation. Then, gradually develop and elaborate on this foundation.

Note: eighth and sixteenth notes on the hi-hat can be played either "straight" up and down, or with a lilt (i.e., lightly swung).

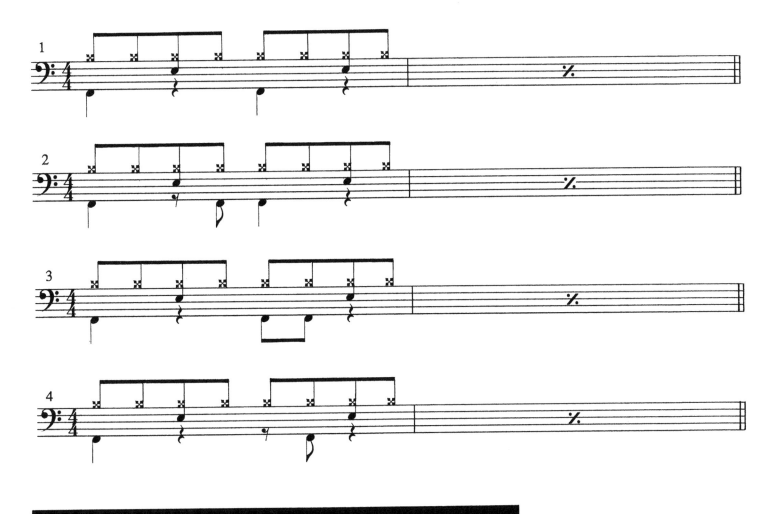

Hear (imagine) sixteenth notes in your head, as played (for example) by a rhythm guitar. In other words, don't try to fly in sixteenth-note syncopations out of the blue; give yourself an internal reference point. This will ensure accuracy and consistency. Hear what you are playing!

In the next two exercises a pardiddle figure is being played between the snare and bass drum.

With the advent of beat and hip-hop and rap music, and the drum machine's presence, a new drumming style and challenge has emerged. Basically, up until recently, multiple bass drum beats were heard primarily in a drum solo (e.g. Buddy Rich/Louie Bellson) setting. Now, there is another place for multiple sixteenth-note beat playing on the bass drum.

Try to play these kinds of figures as evenly as possible. Relax. And practice!

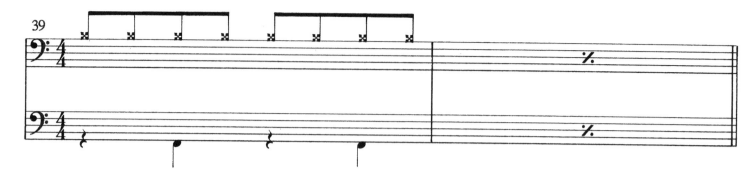

If the tempo is not too fast, sixteenth notes on the ride cymbal or hi-hat can be played with just the right hand.

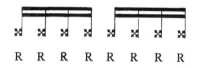

R   R   R   R   R   R   R   R

For faster tempos, you can use alternate stickings on the hi-hat.

R   L   R   L   R   L   R   L

Try other sticking combinations; **the beat will lay differently each way.**

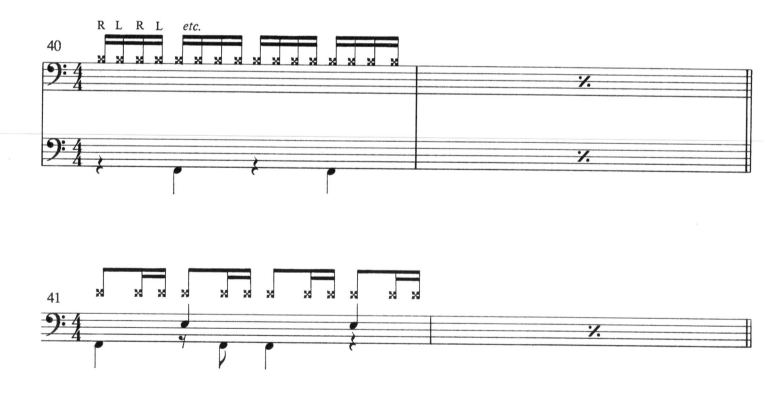

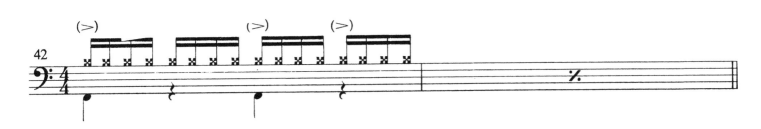

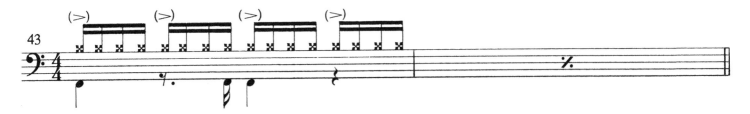

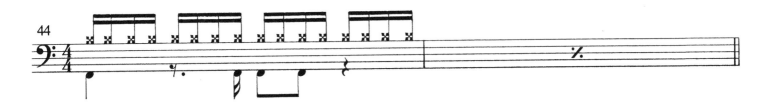

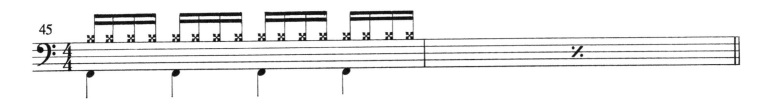

The following beat M.M.=112, is played on "Beirut," from the album
Magnetic, by Steps Ahead.

"Sumo," M.M. = 90, from same album.

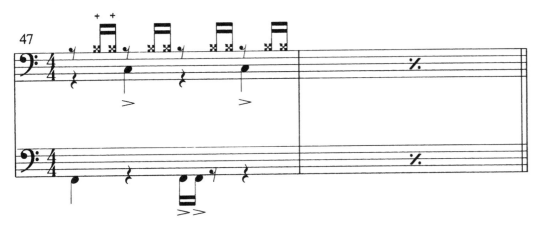

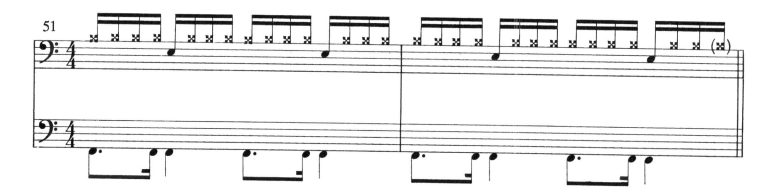

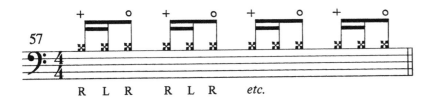

Beats incorporating the use of opening and closing the hi-hat.

R L R   R L R   *etc.*

Note: To help ensure rhythmic accuracy when playing the above rhythm, you may want to ghost the last sixteenth note of each beat with the left hand. Therefore, the rhythm can be executed as:

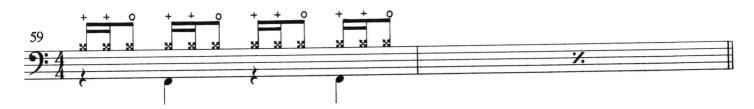

R L R (L) R L R (L)´ *etc.*

(Keep the hi-hat open when playing the ghost notes.)

Practice playing the hi-hat (opening and closing) in combination with the bass drum or with the snare drum, or open and close it by itself.

You can keep the hi-hat open for varying lenths of time. (♪ ♪ ♩ , or whatever.)

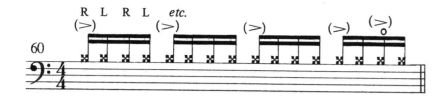

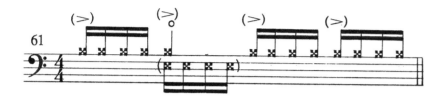

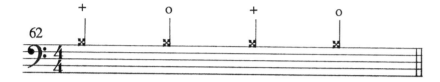

"Can't You See (You Doin' Me Wrong)," from Tower of Power, *Back To Oakland* (Warner Bros.), played by Dave Garibaldi

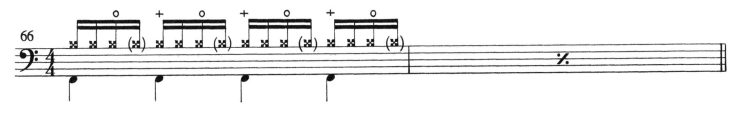

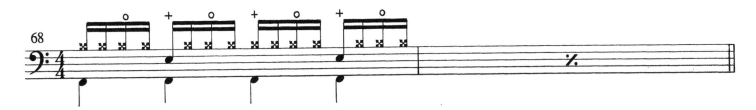

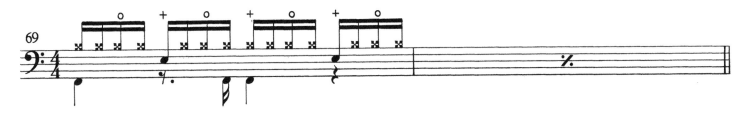

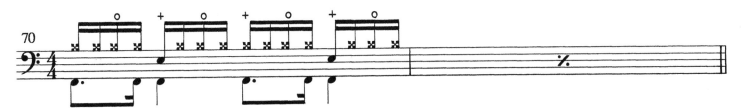

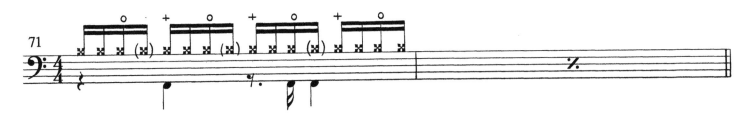

"Oops," from Steps Ahead, *Modern Times* (Elektra/Musician), by Mike Mainieri.
M.M. = 88

Examples of End Bar/Phrase Fills

Re: Double strokes on the bass drum, and the drum speaking: Do not play double strokes too fast (rush), so as to obscure the pulse of the two beats. Sometimes, slower can actually sound faster.

REMINDER: Fills can take you up to the downbeat of the next bar or phase, OR can extend beyond the downbeat. For example:

The way I think of music, once a drummer starts playing time, that's like a golden thread that is woven through the entire tune. That thread should be unbroken. There has to be a continuity of musical thought, even if the tune consciously changes style or tempo. So a fill has to continue what has gone before and lead into what is going to follow. Whatever you want to make out of that is your statement. I prefer to think of it as going along the same path, rather than as taking a detour.

You can make some analogies between music and sports. If we look at music in an ensemble context, which is what bands are, then we're looking at a team. In basketball, let's say, if you get the ball, the object is to advance the ball down the court and get a basket. You can either advance the ball by dribbling it yourself, or by passing it to someone else. If you were in the Harlem Globetrotters, though, you might just stand there and spin the ball on your fingers. That might be good for entertainment, but you're not advancing anything forward. So that's akin to the music stopping for an extended drum solo. That can have its place, but certainly fills shouldn't be show stoppers. They should continue the progress of what the tune is trying to do.

So fills are merely another way to keep time; you can't isolate them out of the context of timekeeping. A fill is like the landscape of the drummer opening up a little bit. Not only is the drummer playing a little bit more, but generally the rest of the band is playing a little bit less right there. You're not just playing a lot of stuff on top of everybody else. The concept is that there's a hole there, so you "fill" it. It could be a very simple little thing, or it could even be space. One of the most effective fills I ever heard was by Buddy Rich: He was playing, and then he suddenly stopped. He used silence, and it was very effective. You've got to remember that the spaces between the notes are just as effective as the notes themselves.

"The notes I handle no better than many pianists. But the pauses between the notes — ah, that is where the art resides!"
    —Arthur Schnabel, *Chicago Daily News*, June 11, 1958.

For popular music (especially in recording work) try to keep the backbeat "clean."
Ghost and filler notes are often not appropriate for this context.

Beat with ghost notes on the snare:

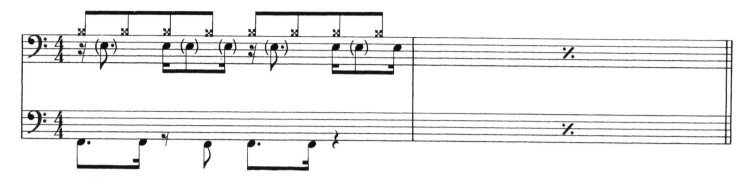

That does not work very well in commercial context — too busy.

Same beat with sixteenth notes on the hi-hat:

This works well in commercial context; it still has sixteenth motion.

Fundamental version of the same beat:

This works well in commercial context — very simple.

Orchestration of a beat:

Backbeat on the snare drum.

Backbeat on the bass drum (suggests a reggae feel).

Reggae

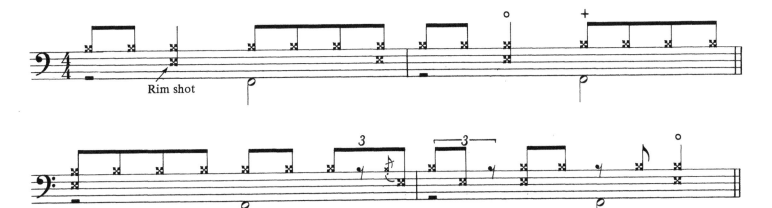

Rim shot

A Sly Dunbar type of beat:

Samba

Authentic Samba is in a "two" feel (which can be notated as 2/4, 2/2, or cut time). Here, let's think of the Samba in a slow to moderate 2/4 meter, with the accent on the second beat. The phrasing of the Samba will vary with the choice of syncopation and accents — that is, the variation of the eight sixteenth notes in the bar.

The following are some authentic Samba rhythms. Remember to accent on beat 2.

My friend, the brilliant Brazilian pianist Eliane Elias, is fond of pointing out that most Americans play (and think of) Samba the wrong way. This is wrong:

This is the correct way to think of Samba:

(For our purposes, I have notated the following examples in cut time.)

Samba snare drum rhythms:

Note: I like to play the following examples with these bass drum rhythms:

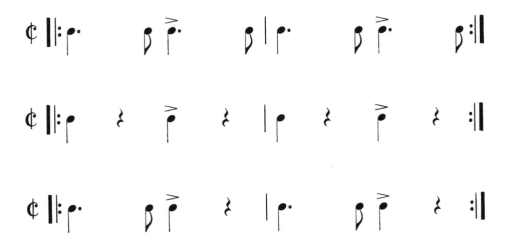

Snare drum (play gracefully):

Improvise on the snare drum. Listen to authentic Brazilian music, or Brazilian influenced drummers (such as Airto) for ideas and inspiration.

Snare and Ride Cymbal can also play accented rhythms, etc., in unison.

Brush/Stick combination: The right-hand eighth-note pattern is often played on the snare drum with a brush. In addition, try this: (M.M. = 158)

Swirl the quarter note.

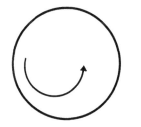

I picked this up from Grady Tate, and used it on "My Ship" from my first solo album.

Jazz and American popular music assimilates the music of other cultures. If you keep the conception and feeling of authentic 2/4 Samba in mind and spirit, then you can retain Samba's authenticity while playing in the 4/4 realm.

Bossa Nova

Baião

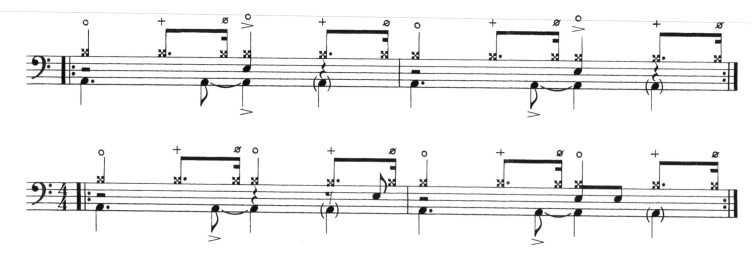

Try the snare drum on the downbeat. The above snare rhythms are merely suggestions. Use your ears. (I've used this rhythm, a modified Baião, on a couple of recordings — notably on the title track of Jaco Pastorius' *Invitation*, M.M. half-note = 160!)

Samba and Samba/Rock

As I talked about earlier, I hear different levels of time in a lot of the music that I play.
For instance, when doing Samba or Samba/rock (or "fusion," if you will), the bass drum
is playing

Bass Drum

and the hi-hat is playing

Hi-Hat

Now, instead of a Samba rhythm on the snare drum

Snare Drum (basic beat)

consider playing a half-time backbeat:

etc.

or

On the ride cymbal, if the tempo is not too fast, I could play

Ride Cymbal (moderate tempo) (or Closed Hi-Hat)

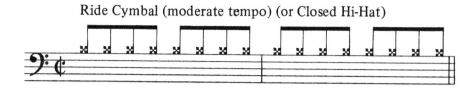

Or maybe I will play a straight eighth-note interpretation of the jazz ride-cymbal pattern:

Ride Cymbal (faster tempo)

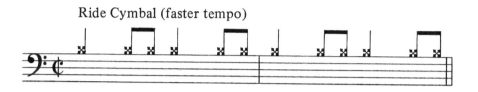

I could also just play quarter notes.

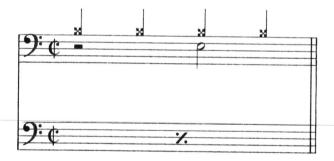

The different levels of time really become apparent when you play half notes on the ride cymbal. I like to play these on the bell of the cymbal. First, play this:

Now, this:

The bell tone really cuts through. Then take it back into:

And then go to offbeats:

That's real exciting; it makes it alive.

Here are some extensions of that same idea:

I played that beat on the Weather Report recording of "Black Market," on the *8:30* album
(M.M. = 120)

The idea behind these variations is that you're not just playing the same beat over and over. But the only reason that this stuff works is because of what I stated earlier about the underlying strength of the basic beat: The knowledege and strength you gain from playing basic beats successfully support any variations or embellishments.

As we move through this text, we discover a very important thing: Experience is working for us. The more that we experience in terms of good, solid, basic timekeeping, the better our chances are of making a more complex beat feel good.

Authentic vs. Creative Generic

When we use Latin/American influences in modern music (whether it be jazz, rock, pop, or whatever), or try to play Latin music outright, we are dealing with a question of authenticity versus what I call "creative generic" — the level of authenticity or creativity depending on the drummer. The more you listen to authentic music, of course, the better your understanding of it will be. But when you are playing Sambas, Rumbas, or whatever, you don't have to be limited to "This is the beat, there is only one way to play it, and that's all there is to it." When you are first learning a rhythm, perhaps it is good to play it authentically, but ultimately the bottom line is whether it sounds good in the context that you're playing in. One way to make a rhythm come alive is with creative variations (accents, orchestrations, etc.), which make the rhythm reflect *you*. It's like using interesting adjectives, or adding spices to food. Music is a reflection of culture. There isn't just one culture in the world, and that's what makes the world so dynamic. So if your music has its own particular accent, that's a good thing.

In much of this music that we're addressing, we are dealing with ostinatos: rhythmic patterns that we repeat and work off of. An ostinato can be something authentic (such as clave), or it can be your own variation. The point is that you have a constant that sets up the music. Then, while weaving this thread through the music, you make your statements. Just like any valid art form (good music, good drama), there's going to be interpretation. So these rhythms and patterns are just to open the door to the realm of possibilities. **Listening to authentic rhythms is encouraged**, but if you hear a rhythm you like and you want to add a note, subtract a note, change the accents, or whatever, go ahead and do it.

Clave

Clave defines the outline of a rhythmic pattern in Afro-Latin musics. There are two common forms of clave — 3/2 clave

Clave

or a variation of that

and 2/3 clave

(Reverse Clave)

The clave, or sense of clave, is always present, whether it is actually played or not — in other words, be aware of a song or rhythm's clave structure. As I play variations of Latin rhythms, I am using the clave as a constant source of reference.

Latin Beats

When asked to play a "Latin feel," I often use beats such as these:

Note: The following Latin rhythms may be played as follows:

Right Hand: Bell of cymbal (or in lighter situations, the ride part of cymbal)
                Closed hi-hat
                Cowbell (look and listen for high and low tones)
                Shell of floor tom (a nice wood sound)

Left Hand: Cross stick on snare drum
                Combination snare/rim (timbale-like)
                Tom-toms

Play H.H. (w/foot)
Short ⎯⎯× and long ⎯⎯×⎯
(closed   (open)

The rhythm shown in examples I and J is known as the Mozambique, or Comparsa. It can be played as written, or — as I sometimes like to do — played as flams where the coinciding beats are circled (right-hand lead: played on cowbell or the shell of the floor tom; left hand on snare and toms, accented). Playing unison beats as flams has the effect of "widening up" the beat — that is, making it more open, and putting that space between the, heretofore, unison beats. Sometimes I like to do that; other times, I enjoy a good, solid *unison* beat between two drums — no flams.

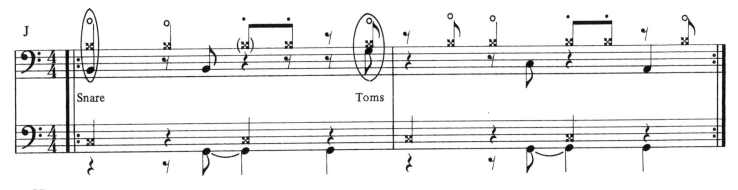

or

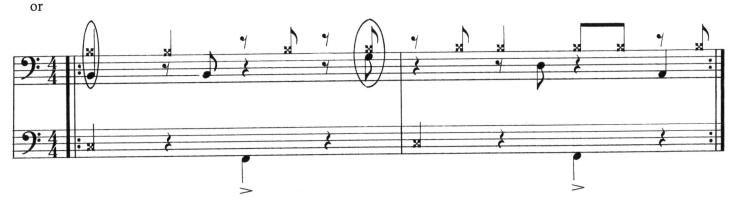

The Abañico

Guillermo Baretto, drummer and timbalist, from Havana, Cuba showed me the correct way to play the Abañico. You always hear that timbale fill (that can be played on a high-pitched tom-tom, or snare drum with snares off) in Latin music.

POOLS

(first 22 measures) M.M. $\frac{1}{2}$ = 86
by Don Grolnick
Steps Ahead

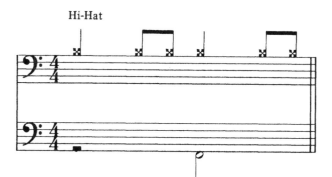

Hi-Hat

Tenor Solo (Basic Beat)
butt end of stick on rim of S.D.

cross stick

Bass Solo (Basic Beat)

Ride
Cymbal

Vibes Solo—Beginning (Basic Beat)

Vibes Solo—End (Basic Beat)

BOTH SIDES OF THE COIN
(first 16 measures) M.M. half-note = 119
by Michael Brecker
Steps Ahead

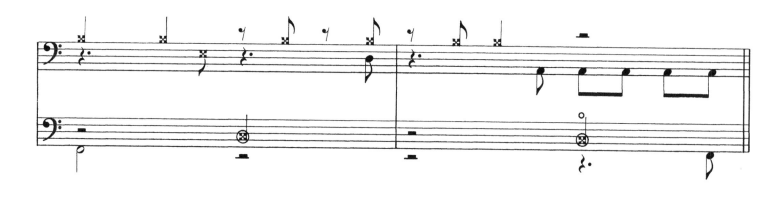

OOPS

(first 17 measures) M.M. = 88
by Michael Mainieri
Modern Times, by Steps Ahead

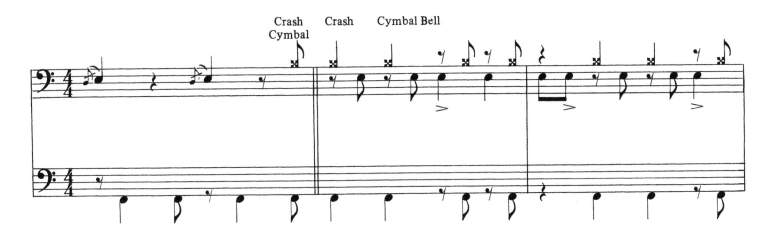

etc.

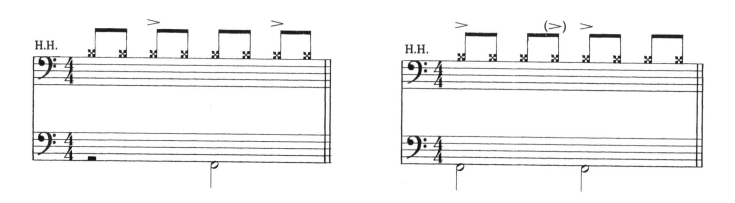

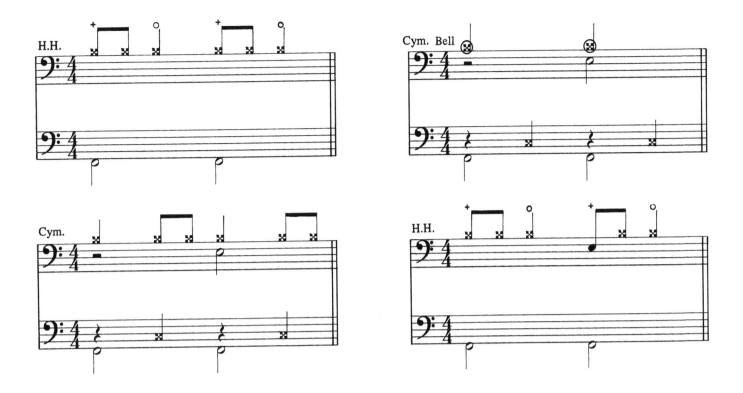

VOLCANO FOR HIRE
(Introduction) M.M. = 134
by Josef Zawinul
Weather Report
FLOOR TOM

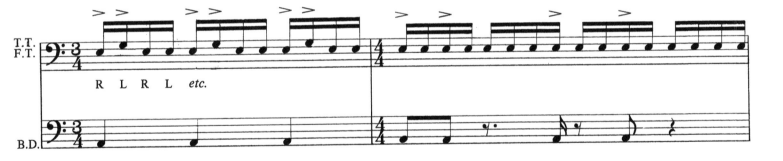

R L R L *etc.*

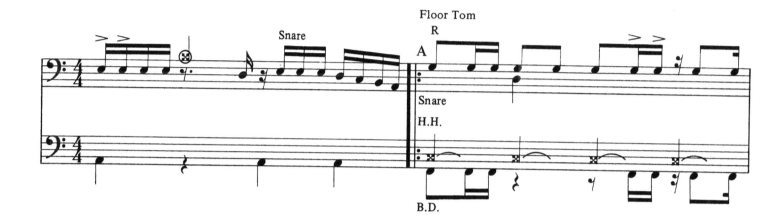

NIGHT PASSAGE

(Introduction) M.M. = 166
by Josef Zawinul
Night Passage, by Weather Report

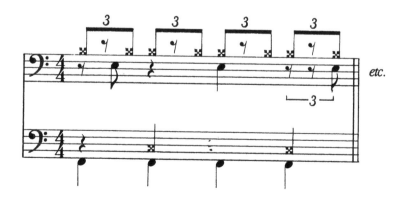

ROCKIN' IN RHYTHM
(Introduction) M.M. = 224
by Duke Ellington
Night Passage, by Weather Report

BROWN STREET
 M.M. = 116
by Josef Zawinul/Wayne Shorter
8:30, by Weather Report

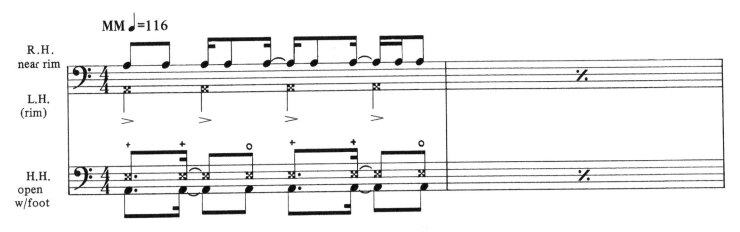

THE PURSUIT OF THE WOMAN IN THE FEATHERED HAT
 M.M. = 108
by Josef Zawinul
Mr. Gone, by Weather Report

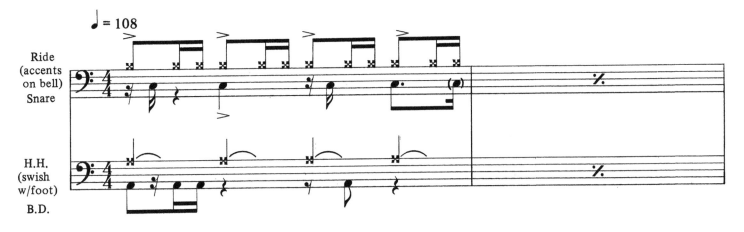

CLINT
M.M. = 118
by John Abercrombie, Marc Johnson and Peter Erskine
Current Events, by John Abercrombie Trio

SAMURAI HEE HAW
M.M. = 166
by Marc Johnson
Bass Desires

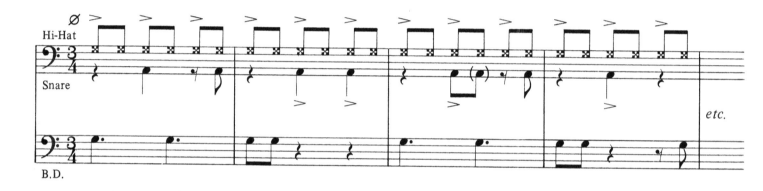

THANKS AGAIN
M.M. = 92
by John Scofield
Bass Desires

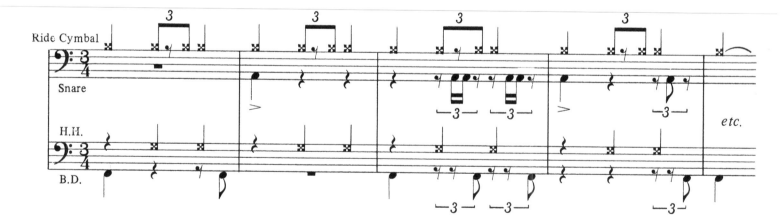

PAPA LIPS

med. Calypso — M.M. half note = 98
by Bob Mintzer
Papa Lips, by Bob Mintzer Big Band

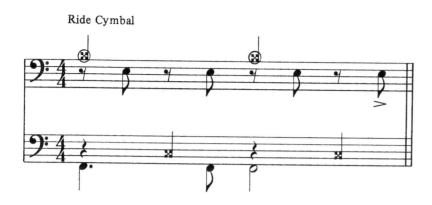

SELF PORTRAIT
M.M. = 70
by Mike Mainieri
Modern Times, by Steps Ahead

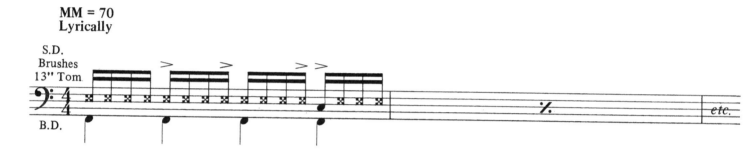

BEIRUT

M.M. = 112
by M.Brecker, M.Mainieri, P. Erskine, C. Loeb and V. Bailey
Magnetic, by Steps Ahead

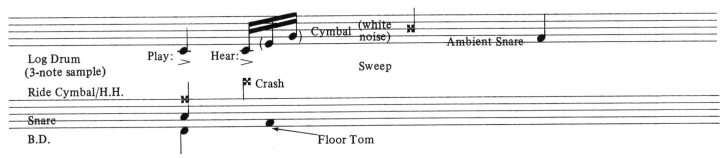

Shuffle

There are several ways to play a shuffle rhythm: the cymbal may play quarter-notes while the snare drum plays the shuffle rhythm

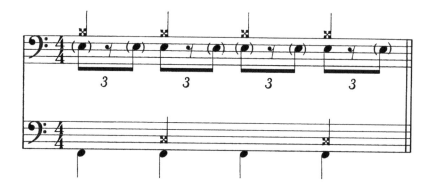

or the cymbal may play the standard ride pattern while the snare plays this backbeat

or this shuffle

or the cymbal and snare may play the shuffle rhythm together.

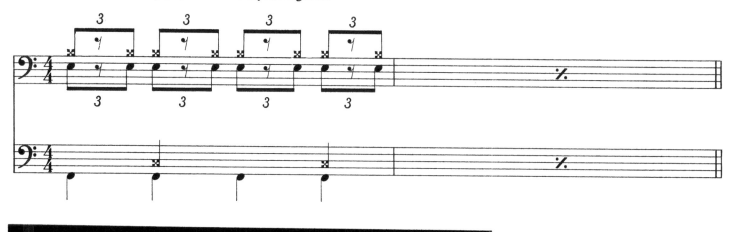

Usually, the bass drum plays on each quarter-note beat with the hi-hat on beats 2 and 4.

A rock 'n' roll shuffle will typically be played stronger (a good, strong backbeat and loud bass drum), and may be played on the ride cymbal or the closed hi-hat.

Rock Shuffle:

The parenthesized snare notes represent the filler beats that are played somewhat like "ghost" notes in between the more fundamental beats (e.g., the backbeat).

Some good examples of the shuffle can be found on traditional blues albums, or on recordings with the Thad Jones/Mel Lewis big band. On the Weather Report album **8:30**, I played a shuffle on the cut "Birdland," with the shuffle rhythm in the bass drum.

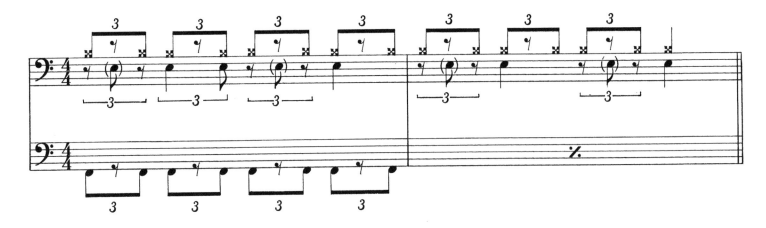

Here are two more medium tempo shuffles — good for rock or blues playing:

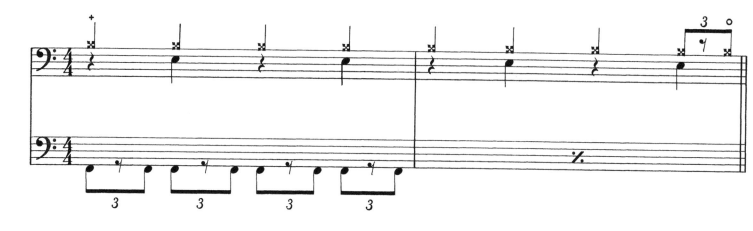

BRUSHES

Playing the drums with brushes is a satisfying experience, and need not be restricted to ballads, the beginnings of standards, or the accompaniment to bass solos. We use brushes because we don't want the attack of the stick. We want a more gentle sound, and generally a more legato sound (especially on ballads). This involves moving the brush across the drumhead in a gentle, legato, and elegant manner. You don't so much go tap, tap, tap with the brushes (unless you specifically want to), but the idea on a ballad is to play pretty.

You also have to understand the flow of the music. If it's a slow, triplet feel, you have to be careful not to imply double time. So you have to be consistent with the way you're phrasing and playing.

Technique

As a starting point, we're dealing with circular motion on the drumhead. The hands generally move in opposite and contrary directions. The way I personally play is by moving my left hand counterclockwise and my right hand clockwise. Many drummers, in fact, play the other way. (But since this is *my* drum book, I'm going to show you the way I do it!)

In diagram number one, we see that the left hand is rotating counterclockwise, and the right hand clockwise. If you imagine the snare drum as being the face of a clock, the left-hand circle is located between 7:00 and 8:00, and the right-hand circle between 1:00 and 2:00. In the first exercise, practice giving one rotation per pulse with each hand. Start the rotation at the top of each hand's circle. You'll notice that there's not too much point to the beat; you don't hear each pulse as it's occuring (it's very subtle). This is okay for now. Just make sure that you get as smooth a rotation as possible. Don't push or "swish" the beat.

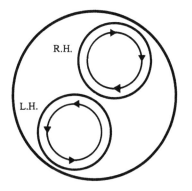

Now we're going to apply some articulation to this. The left hand will continue the smooth, counterclockwise circles. But lift the right hand just as it completes its revolution, and gently tap on the drumhead at the beginning of the next circle. In other words, the right hand will attack at 12:00, and lift just prior to that — at 10:00 or 11:00 — so that the right brush stays on the head for as long as possible before articulating the next quarter-note pulse. (Note: My right-hand fulcrum is between my thumb and the first joint of my middle finger. Articulation is achieved by a lifting of the brush accompanied by an opening and closing of the grip.)

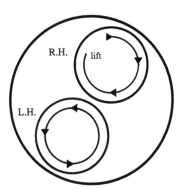

This quarter-note brush pulse is quite effective and will work in a number of musical situations and circumstances.

In order to play the traditional jazz ride rhythm, the left hand continues as it's done before. Meanwhile, the right hand will articulate the beginning of the first revolution, articulate the second, and then in the midst of the second, you must lift the brush and articulate the "a" of 2 (if you're thinking "1 & a 2 & a etc."). This articulation is more of a glancing blow, as opposed to an up-and-down, stick-like movement. Care and effort should be taken to make this sound as smooth as possible.

For faster tempos, the left hand movement will have to be minimized. This can be done by having the brush travel a shorter distance (smaller circumference), or moving it back and forth / left-to-right (45 degree angle), or by halving (in time) the circular motion. For the best uptempo brush playing, listen to recordings made by Philly Joe Jones.

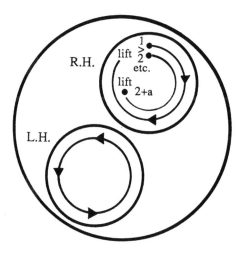

The next diagram shows the "over and under" movement; that is, the hands and brushes literally go over and under each other. The brushes are moving in the same basic directions as before, but we're moving the brushes over a larger area of the drumhead, creating more texture and inflection within this basic quarter-note pulse. Again, the right brush articulates each pulse by tapping the head lightly. To connect these pulses in a smooth and legato manner, I quickly swirl the brush, first dragging it momentarily across the surface, then rotating it slightly and rapidly. It is a subtle movement.

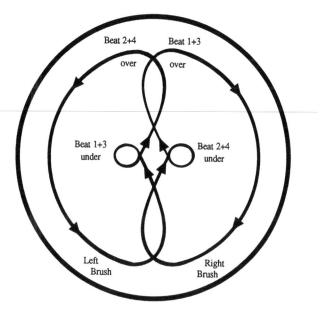

It is possible (and desirable) to articulate rhythms outside the quarter-note pulse with either hand. Practice doing that.

As I mentioned before, when you are playing a slow triplet feel, you have to be careful not to imply double time. However, there are times when you *want* to change to a double-time feel (at the bridge, for example). I often will double-time the brush pattern while keeping the hi-hat in the original 4/4 meter — the 2 and 4 become 3 in the new tempo. In other words, not a full-tilt double time.

Note: Brushes play double time, while the Hi-Hat's tempo remains the same (the "old" 2+4).

Straight Eighth-Note Music

Don't forget that brushes sound great on straight eighth-note music as well! That includes Bossa Novas, Sambas, and all sorts of Latin music, as well as rock, pop, and bluegrass. Did I forget country and western?

Equipment

I now use Vic Firth's *Jazz Rakes* for brushes — they are the first nylon brush that I've preferred over wire. Their textural and handling qualities make them unique. They play and sound real good.

For playing where I'd like more articulation and louder dynamic characteristics, I use the Calato Ed Thigpen model brushes. These are also made of nylon, but of a thicker and coarser type than the *Jazz Rakes* – they are great for cymbal playing, as well as for all types of ethnic musics: samba, calypso, etc. I also occasionally like to use Pro-Mark's *Multi-Rods*, which are tightly bound thin wooden dowels. All of these tools are like the brushes and colors of an artist's palette for the drummer.

PRACTICE

The idea of quality versus quantity is a universal axiom. A lot of times, I don't get the chance to practice (or I have the chance but don't take advantage of it). Professional working situations can keep you on the run, but the plus side of that, of course, is that you're getting to play everyday. There's no substitute for playing experience, and by playing experience I mean *playing with other musicians*. No one can make a career out of playing drums in the basement. The drums are an ensemble creature: We have to interact with other musicians. This is the true joy of drumming. While it is fun to play the drums in a solo setting, that's not going to be the bulk of the playing situations that you're going to be in.

In practice, then, you should prepare yourself for ensemble situations. Practice timekeeping. In addition, you do have to work on your chops, which means practicing basic snare drum techniques. I find it helpful to work out of books such as George Lawrence Stone's *Stick Control*, the Bower book, and the Podemski book (which was very useful in my training). You must also work on the basic rudiments, and on understanding your hand grips — how they work and how to optimize your particular grip. You must understand such things as the degree of relaxation or tension in your grip, the angle and access of your wrists, the positioning of your fingers, and where the fulcrum of the stick is. There are several methods and disciplines of snare drum technique, but it is not the intent of this book to deal with that. Suffice to say that all drumming is a combination of finger, wrist, and arm motion. During my time of snare drum study and practice in college I concentrated on discovering just how much of each I was using, and trying to weed out the bad habits. We want to make our drumming motion and activity as efficient as possible to get the most out of what we do, and this frees us up to make that much more music.

When I went back to college (after three years on the road with Stan Kenton's band), I was having a guilt problem because I felt that I wasn't practicing enough. My teacher wasn't pressuring me, because he sensed that I was going through a certain transitional period. But at one point he said to me, "You know, I've got kids here who practice seven or eight hours a day, but that doesn't impress me. If you would practice fifteen minutes a day and accomplish something, then you're doing more than someone who is just putting in time at the instrument for seven or eight hours." Spending time on your instrument is important; a number of hours per day or per week can increase your proficiency. But if you are not careful, it can also increase your level of bad habits. It's the *musical* practice hours that really count. Recently, I've felt that the benefits from my hours of musical practice are enormous. The rapport I'm developing with my instrument — it's like we're the best of friends. It's not just the result of the sheer hours that I slaved away. It's because of the musical practice that I've done.

As important as it is to isolate certain things and practice them, whenever you practice, you must PRACTICE MUSIC. Every time you play your instrument, PLAY MUSIC on it. You've got to discipline yourself to do that. Think of it as QUALITY vs. QUANTITY.

When I sit down to practice the drumset, the first thing I'll do is start playing time. Then I'll play something in the context of time, in that musical style that I'm working in. When I play time, I have an internal reference. I start to create and build something out of a motivic idea, which can be generated out of timekeeping, whether it's in the realm of swing, Samba, or something funky, or whatever. When I play something funky, for example, I immediately start thinking of a rhythm guitar as a musical reference point. It might not be anything specific; I just draw on everything I've ever listened to. It will be combined in different ways every time I sit down. But there's a musical reference point I draw on. I don't just play in a vacuum.

We each hear certain types of music, and certain beats, at particular tempos. I guess that has something to do with our metabolism and our heartbeat. But as drummers, we have to be able to play anywhere in the whole spectrum of tempos, from very slow to very fast. So when I sit down to play, I first play at a tempo that feels comfortable to me. We all have a certain median tempo, just like we have a certain pace when we walk. Some days I walk faster, and some days I walk slower. But a musician has to be able to do things at different speeds, so I will then pick out different tempi at which to play different grooves.

Anything you practice, be sure to practice at all dynamic levels and at all different tempos. I think it's invaluable to record yourself. The tape does not lie. It gives you the best feedback and input as to how you're playing. Sometimes you can listen to a recording of yourself, and listen to it like it's any drummer. Does it feel good? It's generally possible to be objective when listening to yourself on tape (try not to be so wrapped up or enamored by the fact that you're listening to yourself). If it sounds good, celebrate that. If it doesn't sound good, try to figure out why it doesn't sound or feel good.

The other kind of feedback that's very valuable is visual — using a mirror. How do you sit when you play the drumset? Are you hunched over? Do you sit straight? Is your posture good? Are your shoulders drawn up or are you relaxed? Do you move around too much? When you move, do you move in jerky motions or do you move smoothly? This will all translate into how the music sounds (and vice versa). The way the music sounds is visually revealed by the way you move. Both tape and visual forms of feedback are very important. A mirror is an economical way to see yourself play. Video is becoming so available and commonplace, if not in the private home then most certainly in schools, that the drummer should check himself out this way. I've learned a lot doing this.

When you are practicing, if something is giving you difficulty, be sure to practice it slowly. You will be able to figure out just about anything if you practice it slowly enough. And then be sure not to change tempos capriciously. Don't speed up and slow down relative to the music's difficulty. In other words, it's a common mistake to slow down when something gets difficult, and to speed back up when it gets easier. But be sure to maintain constant tempos; that's an important discipline.

Practicing with a metronome is a very good idea. You should use an electronic metronome with a headphone output so that you can listen to the metronome through headphones. This, of course, resembles working with a click track, which is something that you will have to be able to do if you want to do any professional recording. If you've never played with a click it can be quite awkward and challenging. Ralph Humphrey put it this way — about "chasing" the click — when he advised "don't play too much on top of the click. Just try to relax and play right along with it, so you hear the click." You'll be treating it then as part of the rhythm section.

The following are basic stroke, rudimental and warm-up exercises. Warm-up exercises are always a good idea.

All drumming is made up of three basic strokes:

1. **The single stroke**
2. **The double stroke**
3. **The flam**

Below are some of the essential drumming rudiments that you should be able to play. It's a good idea to practice rudiments on the drumset, i.e., between the snare and toms (over a bass drum/hi-hat ostinato) to increase your proficiency in moving around the kit.

Single Stroke Roll

Double Stroke Roll

5 Stroke Roll

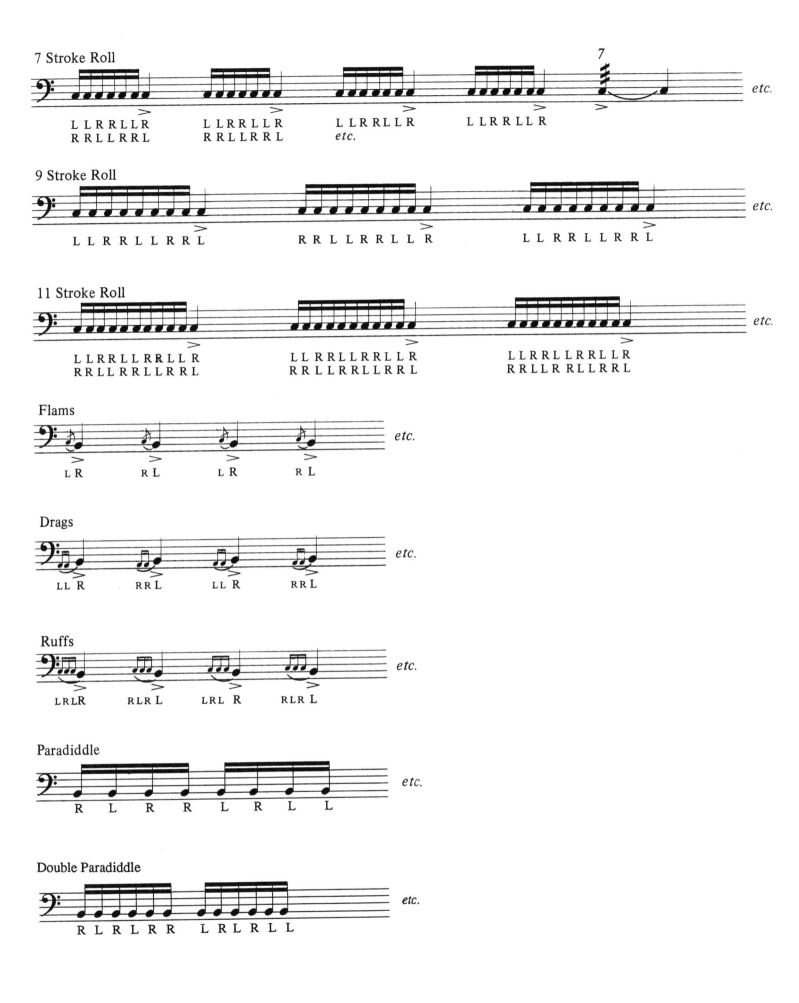

My Personal Warm-Up Routine

(shown to me by Prof. George Gaber of Indiana University)

Right Hand

Left Hand

etc.

I also alternate single strokes, double strokes, and paradiddles at the same tempo and dynamic level (with no accents). Try to attain as even a pulse as possible.

etc.

R R L L R R L L R L R L R L R L R L R L R R L R L L

Start playing all of the above at a moderate tempo, and then gradually increase the speed.
Then try playing them at a slow tempo.
Play at different dynamic levels:
Slow to Fast
Soft to Loud
and anywhere in between. This is what control is all about.

In addition to these warm-up exercises, I will stretch my limbs and hands, and sometimes shake my hands loose. It feels like I get the blood flowing and the joints lubricated — non-stress exercises (it's not really exercise, but it feels like it gets everything loosened up).
When I was with Weather Report, it could be a real strenuous job, and the band would hit it from the moment we went on stage. So right before we went on stage I would do 100 jumping jacks, and maybe twenty-five sit-ups and push-ups. I would do stretching exercises, and then I'd run in place for five minutes, just to get all pumped up and get the blood moving, because most of the time playing a Weather Report concert was like playing in a football game.

PHRASING

As I mentioned in the chapter on practice, the first thing I do when I practice is play time, and I always have an internal reference point (such as the sound of a rhythm guitar). Now, as regards to phrasing, when I play time, I'm thinking of the clock, and I'm aware of what the subdivisions are so that as I play, I'm not flying in beats out of the blue. It's not guesswork; the beats fit into the clock that's moving. So when you practice, you always have to think in terms of the music — what it is you're playing and what it sounds like in a musical application. It can be specific or not, but you have to give yourself a musical reference — some sort of time base. Even if you get more advanced and are playing "free," there's still a clock going. It might speed up or slow down, but it's not like there's NO clock, because you send every beat you play out into space with a certain velocity behind it. It propels. To the other musicians and listeners, there's a dynamic element — an ebb and flow; there's physical energy, and a time base from which that is born.

When I play time, I don't have to give myself a big count-off. I can just start — boom. I give myself an upbeat and I've got the quarter-note pulse going from that upbeat onward. The time is moving forward, and immediately I'm defining the subdivisions. If it's jazz, the 8th notes are swung. So the subdivisions I'm thinking of are all of the swung upbeats. Since the quarter-note pulse is fundamental, I hear a walking bass line. If it's something funky, then I hear a rhythm guitar in my head. If it's Samba, I feel it in two, and I hear an acoustic guitar playing Samba rhythm, and maybe a surdo, which provides the pulse. So I hear components of a particular muscial style that have to do with the subdivisions of the time. By doing that, everything has to fall in the right place! Once I have that musical context established (which I do from the first note), then if I want to play something over the bar line, the knowledge is there of where the time is. But if I don't have time established, and I try to play something over the top of it, it's not going to sound good. IF I DON'T HAVE A REFERENCE POINT INTERNALLY, THEN I CAN'T EXTERNALIZE IT MUSICALLY AND EXPECT IT TO SOUND GOOD, OR EXPECT THE REST OF THE BAND TO BE ABLE TO KEY INTO IT.

A beat should have a certain elegance. When I talk about subdivisions, I don't mean to imply a purely mechanical thing. It has to be human, and it has to be warm. A good example is the difference between the way American musicians sing Samba, and the way Brazilians sing it (Brazilians are more flowing). It has something to do with the difference between the English and Portugese languages: Their music is soft, round, and it moves forward. It has a lot of energy; it also has a sway to it. (I like to think of a beat as being strong and solid, while at the same time having sunlight, or a fresh breeze, coming through it.)

The thing that moves music forward is tension and release. So when you're moving the pulse forward, the tension and release come from what you do on top of that: the subdivisions. You get more and more into the "rubber-banding" of playing on top of or behind the beat. What's always neglected in conversations about playing on top or behind is that **there is a beat**. There's an **absolute** about where the time is. Not everybody can play on top of the beat, because that would then become the reference point; that would *be* the beat. Time is just like pitch: There's a center to it, and if you get above or below it, that creates some of the tension. This whole discussion of ahead of or behind the beat is tricky. It messes with the heads of a lot of drummers, because they worry about whether they are on top of the beat or behind it. **Just play the time and concentrate on making it feel good.**

READING

First of all, you have to know note values, how to differentiate between them, and how to piece them together quickly, so that in a sight-reading situation, you're not sitting there wondering about the difference between a dotted 8th note and a regular 8th note. The basic drum books such as the Bower *Imperial Method* or Louie Bellson's 4/4 reading text are terrific, because they get you used to seeing different rhythms written out, and you can use them to sharpen your sight-reading edge. A great idea is to take the simpler rhythmic exercises for snare drum, and play (sight-read) them at as FAST a tempo as is possible. And then try the same thing, with both hands UNISON — NO FLAMS.

The most important element in sight-reading DRUMSET music is your ears. What's written down on paper is not always the gospel. A lot of interpretation may be involved, whether it's the stage band at school, one of your friends who wrote a chart, a jingle, or a film date. They're just writing approximations of what they want. The nature of contemporary music and drumming is that there is an element of spontaneous playing and interaction going on.

The drum part basically tells you how long the piece of music is, what dynamics you want to be aware of, and it gives you some basic rhythmic figures. The rhythmic figures that are written above the staff are basically what some part of the ensemble is playing. It's up to the drummer's discretion whether to catch it or not. If it's written within the staff, generally it's a good bet that you will be expected to play that. Some people write very specific things — a snare drum here, a tom-tom there. To prove that you're a good sight-reader, you'll try to hit, or "cut" everything the first time through. But I've stopped doing that, because if you catch every rhythmic figure, you'll sound like a circus or show drummer. If you've got 14 horn players, or just two synthesizer players and a guitarist hitting a chord, that might have enough impact by itself. There's no reason why the drummer has to catch it, too (unless he wants to). Consider, also, what do you catch where? Are you moving it along, or not? A lot of drummers catch everything, and hit everything on the drumkit, and that's a deadly sort of punctuation, because it stops everything. It's like stepping off the curb, landing on both feet, and having to start your stride over. Bass drum is good, or bass drum and cymbal, or snare and cymbal. I like to catch accents with just a crash cymbal. Texturally it's nice. The cymbal speaks (everything doesn't have to be "boom, crash, crunch"). And with fills, you can't play the same doggone fill every time, even if the rhythmic setup is repetitive. So remember: Discretion is the better part of valor — *and sight-reading.*

I pride myself on being a good reader, and I think it's important to practice sight-reading. I like to be able to read anything that's thrown in front of me. And you have to, because the drums are such an important part of any band. You can't be sending out ambiguous signals, either because of a bad choice of fills, or because you don't know what's going on.

One secret of reading is to look at a rhythm and know what it sounds like without having to count it, just as you look at a printed word and recognize it without having to spell it out. When you're sight-reading, you should also make sure that you understand the "road-map": know if there are D.S.'s, D.C.'s, repeats, know if there are any tempo changes, make sure that there aren't any surprises when you turn the page, and things like that. It's a good idea to peruse the music and check for mistakes, such as too many beats in a bar, etc., and use your judgment to amend the part (or, if necessary, ask the writer/leader).

If you're playing something that's been recorded by someone else, you might want to sit down with that recording and the music to find out how that particular drummer interpreted the chart that was written. Another drummer's interpretation is not the final word; it might be great, or it might not be so great — but you could learn from it.

In general recording situations, such as a record date, you might have drum parts. Often you have a master piano score, and it might have a couple of particular things written here or there. You're basically reading from a lead sheet, so you'll see the bass line, harmonic activity, and the basic rhythms. Then you decide when you are going to catch things and when you are going to be the rhythmic constant that these things play off of. It becomes creative reading. You're making decisions. Generally, the better written something is, the easier and quicker it is to get it together. But discretion is the name of that game.

YOU'VE GOT TO BE ABLE TO READ IF YOU WANT TO BE A PROFESSIONAL.

TUNING

General Observations

The sound that a musician hears in his head is connected to his conception; that's why it is so important to become familiar with as much music as possible. The many varieties of recorded music available to you now will offer more than enough opportunities to hear current, "in" drumming sounds, to hear all of the sonic possibilities, and to hear sounds that are stylistically appropriate to the music. Your sound shouldn't be obtrusive, in terms that it's too dry or too ringy. There are no clear-cut rules, except that your ears have to let you know that, "This speaks well, and this doesn't."

The beauty of a drum sound is the tone. I have found that the tuning and sound of the drums I'm playing will greatly affect the way, or stylistic manner, in which I play. For example, tight, high-pitched, double-headed drums, with a small bass drum, automatically propel me in the direction of playing in a style similar to that of, say, Jack DeJohnette, or Tony Williams when he played with Miles Davis. Low-pitched drums tend to make me play in a funkier style. On the other hand, an apparently incongruous drum sound can open up musical possibilities. For example, playing funk on a small "jazz" kit with an 18" bass drum can spark some new ideas.

Bass Drum

For jazz playing, I favor a small, 18", two-headed bass drum, tuned fairly tight, but still with enough low-frequency sound to qualify it as a bass drum. For general and recording purposes, as well as commercial and funky music, I use a larger bass drum with stuffing (a pillow or blanket) against the head, to create a low-frequency, dry sound. A drum like that sounds good over the radio, and it gives a good pulse. If you use a bass drum with a lot of ring, the tone can carry over to the next articulation. So certain types of music don't sound good on a bass drum with a lot of ring to it, whereas other types of music don't sound good on a bass drum that is too dry. Another bass drum sound is the two-headed, low-pitched, larger open drum sound, similar to that of Buddy Rich. There are innumerable tuning and sound possibilities. You must use your ears to decide which one is right for the situation you're in.

Tom-Toms

For jazz playing, I prefer two-headed tom-toms, wide open with no muffling, tuned high to low, creating a spread similar to that found in a choir (soprano, alto, tenor, bass). Again, you must use your ears. For commercial and funk music, I use lower pitched toms, with some muffling, but still allowing for some melodious tone. A lot of times, mounted tom-toms are of a particular pitch or frequency that blots out other things. You might hit a tom-tom and it will seem to clash with a guitar chord, and you will realize that you should have hit a lower tom. You can analyze sound in terms of frequencies, and if everything sort of collides at one certain point, it won't sound very good. That's why, for example, drummers have to be very careful with electronic percussion, like Simmons drums. If the band you're playing with has a lot of synthesizers, and a lot of synthesized drums, all of a sudden you can get this big, middle-band wave of sound. It all becomes a wash after a while. There's no frequency space, so the rhythmic impact gets lost.

Snare Drum

I generally like to play on a medium to high-pitched snare drum. For funk, R&B, pop, or jingle recording work, a snare drum that is tuned fairly low with muffling works best. Avoid extremes in snare tensioning. Check out the difference between wood and metal (aluminum and brass) shells, as well as cast or non-cast rims.

Muffling

There has always been drum muffling, ever since the drumset came into being. However, I don't think that internal mufflers are a good idea — pushing up from the bottom of the head in an isolated spot. Mechanically, they're not efficient, and I don't know how smart it is to have something pushing up against the head when you're striking down on it. Also, they're always breaking and rattling anyway. A little external muffling seems to make a lot more sense, using something like the Yamaha external mufflers, or tape, or the ring-type mufflers such as the mylar-plastic *Zero Rings.*

Actual Tuning

Make sure that the head is properly seated on the shell. Now, pushing your index finger into the center of the drum head about 1/16th", begin to tap around the lugs in order to hear the overtones and see what part of the head is higher or lower than the other. It is important that the head be in tune with itself.

Experience tells you that the top head is where you go for fine tuning and touch response. After each head is in tune with itself, the trick is to get one tensioned relative to the other. The bottom head has a lot of effect in determining pitch. If the bottom is too slack or tight, particularly on the larger drums, it chokes the sound. As a general rule, avoid extremes in muffling, tuning, and going for certain pitches.

Heads

I use a variety of Evans' CAD/CAM drum heads: the *Uno* 1000 gauge coated heads on the snare drum batter, with a 300 gauge head on the bottom; on 10 and 12 inch tom batters, I use *Uno* 1000 gauge (for their bright upper range); 13 or 14 inch and larger diameter drums, I'll generally employ Rock (2ply) heads on the batter (for their warmth of sound); all toms have *Resonant Glass* heads on the bottom. For the bass drum, I use the single-ply *Uno* 1000 gauge head.

The Setup

I don't want to pick one setup and say, "This is the only set I'm going to play." I could live with only one, but where does it say that you can't have more than one? So if the drummer can afford it, it's a good idea to have different setups for different situations. Some drummers use 24" bass drums for everything, and feel that they can control the sound. But, for me, in a trio setting, a drum that big is just too loud (also, I like to play on a 4-piece kit in that setting). I want a small bass drum for certain things, a larger one for other things, and a couple of different snare drums — one funky, and one crisper. I'll use either a 4" or a 5 1/2" snare drum for jazz gigs, and for funk I'll use a 5 1/2" or deeper. It's the same with cymbals. The sound is going to affect what you play. A nice, dry K. Zildjian cymbal is different than a bright, splashy A. Zildjian. There can also be very good reasons for using different drumheads in different situations.

Ultimately, it's the sound you get in your head and the touch that you develop with your hands. I heard Buddy Rich play on a wide variety of drumsets, and he still sounded like Buddy, because his identity was so strong and his touch was so good that he could get his sound on any drum. That's what a sound comes down to: It's you. The equipment has to be good, but having a particular setup doesn't guarantee anything.

"I think a snare drum and a tom-tom — the two together — is certainly sufficient for any kind of solo pattern. You could work up an endless variety of combinations with these two components. Add to that a bass drum, and perhaps a floor tom-tom, and that would be a handful in anybody's band. It's simply a matter of how proficient you are. By having more equipment than that, you would simply be able to duplicate what you could already do in a different direction. But it wouldn't mean you were making more music, or playing more of a variety of rhythmic patterns. There are more tones, of course . . . I don't know if the need is really there for an infinite variety of drums. But again, I can only say that it's up to the individual. If one feels that's his need, then by all means he should do so. As long as it's musical. The only thing that justifies it is the music.
. . . I think it would be practical to explore the drumset from a simplistic point of view. One should reach a point of non-expansion, so to speak, before one expands."
— Elvin Jones, *Modern Drummer*, December 1982

"To me, the hi-hat is another ride cymbal. Every cymbal I use is a ride cymbal. Every one of my cymbals is also a crash cymbal. I use only three. Three is enough."
— Mel Lewis, *Modern Drummer*, February 1985

GENERAL PROFESSIONAL ADVICE

With your fellow musicians, it has always been my theory that most musicians generally try to play their best. No one is up there deliberately trying to play badly or sabotage the band. Some musicians may be very self-absorbed in what they're doing, so it seems they're not part of the team, and that might need to be addressed, but you're all up there trying your best — even though you might not be *sounding* your best. That's just the way it goes, so when you're dealing with other musicians, you have to take that into account, and realize that they're human beings. Dirty looks on the bandstand are not going to help anyone play better. You know that *you* don't play better if someone gives you a dirty look, so likewise, a dirty look from you isn't going to make anyone else play better. It just doesn't work that way. Diplomacy is part of my nature, and I think it helps when dealing with musicians, especially because we tend to wear our egos on our sleeves. You can't go around bruising everyone. So when I'm around musicians I respect, I might even be a little self-effacing. I don't go around saying, "Boy, I played terribly," but I'm not afraid to admit that what I played might not have been the right feel for a particular thing. That relaxes the situation so that someone else can say, "Hey, actually what I was doing wasn't so cool," and then you can arrive at a solution because the defenses have been lowered. Of course, at the same time, you have to believe in what you're doing, and play with conviction.

Show up early for every gig. Be there early and ready to go!

Play what the music requires.

Set up so that you can have eye contact with the other musicians.

Keep your instrument in good working condition.

Warm-up

You may be discreet about doing this. It is not necessary to be on the stand playing all over the drumset right before and between a show, or in the studio, where quiet before and between takes can be important. Just make sure that you are comfortably set up. You can loosen your chops up on a pad or padded chair. Or as I do, playing on my thigh above the knee.

Don't play loud. Play relaxed. Start in a medium (tempos) range, and expand outward (slower — faster).

Pay attention to the business side of things!

Stay healthy.

And be honest — with yourself, and others.

"You've got to live, man. You cannot always work. You've got to have fun in life, and then your work is going to be a reflection of that — and vice-versa. Live first: that's what I believe."

— Josef Zawinul, *Keyboard* Magazine, March 1984

More Advice (from some well-known musicians . . .)

"You play the drums, I'll play the guitar."
— John Scofield

"Play that wide, fat beat that I can drive a Mack truck through. I like that."
— Marc Johnson

"Don't play so loud."
— Randy Brecker

"And don't play a fill every two bars."
— Eliane Elias Brecker

"Make me sound good."
— John Abercrombie

"Never pet a burning dog."
— Steve Gadd

"The way I figure it, is that Monk, Bird, Dizzy, and them cats took the music to a higher level, you know? I think it's the highest level of any kind of music. It's the most highly spiritual music because they don't know what they're going to play. It's from the Creator, to the artist, direct to the audience — split second timing. If that isn't spiritual, I don't know what the hell is."

"Freedom without discipline is chaos; you have to have some discipline. Everything you do takes discipline. A lot of young drummers are real good; their reflexes are good and everything, but will they be able to do that when they're 70 years old? Will they have enough discipline? Discipline means to **relax:** *Can they relax? That's what it takes to play the drums."*

"People don't give a s--- how many paradiddles you can play; people only know what they feel. The drum is the second human instrument, the voice being the first. You can take a drum and just move the earth; you can just transport people. **I was taught by Chick Webb that, if you're playing before an audience, you're supposed to take them away from everyday life — wash away the dust of everyday life. And that's all music is supposed to do."**

— Art Blakey, *Modern Drummer*, September 1984

"Another thing about rhythm is that when an artist is performing on his instrument he breathes in his normal fashion. When the artist is breathing improperly, it's like the audience is left with a little case of indigestion. It's like eating a meal in a hurry. Not **swinging** *is like that. It leads to tension in the audience. It's a physical reaction which you give off "*

— Jo Jones, as told to Nat Hentoff, recounted by Chip Stern
   in *Modern Drummer*, January 1984

"We'll start off playing a very simple beat — the basic beat," Papa Jo concluded in his keynote to The Drums album. **"Always start basic and you'll never go wrong . . . after you have control of your instrument, you can do whatever you wish. Regardless of whatever they name it: YOU PLAY."**

SELECTED DISCOGRAPHY

title	w/artist	label
Birthday In Britain	Stan Kenton	Creative World
Fire, Fury and Fun	Stan Kenton	Creative World
New Vintage	Maynard Ferguson	Columbia
Carnival	Maynard Ferguson	Columbia
Montreux Summit	Stan Getz/Bob James	Columbia
Mr. Gone	Weather Report	Columbia
8:30	Weather Report	Columbia
Night Passage	Weather Report	Columbia
Weather Report	Weather Report	Columbia
Mingus	Joni Mitchell	Elektra/Asylum
Michel Colombier	Michel Colombier	Chrysalis
Un Poco Loco	Bobby Hutcherson	Columbia
Cables Vision	George Cables	Contemporary
Sonic Text	Joe Farrell	Contemporary
Relaxin' At Camarillo	Joe Henderson	Contemporary
Peter Erskine	Peter Erskine	Contemporary
Mistral	Freddie Hubbard	Liberty
Word Of Mouth	Jaco Pastorius	Warner Bros.
Invitation	Jaco Pastorius	Warner Bros.
Wanderlust	Mike Mainieri	Warner Bros
To Chi Ka	Kazumi Watanabe	Nippon Columbia
Paradox	Steps	Nippon Columbia
Steps Ahead	Steps Ahead	Elektra/Musician
Modern Times	Steps Ahead	Elektra/Musician
Foxie	Bob James	Columbia
Bop City	Ben Sidran	Antilles
SwinGrass '83	Buell Neidlinger	Antilles
Magic Touch	Stanley Jordan	Blue Note
Train Of Thought	Mitchel Forman	Magenta
Na Pali Coast	Peter Sprague	Concord Jazz
Hearts And Numbers	Don Grolnick	Hip Pocket
Bass Desires	Marc Johnson	ECM
Current Events	John Abercrombie	ECM
Magnetic	Steps Ahead	Elektra
This Is This	Weather Report	Columbia
Transition	Peter Erskine	Denon
Second Sight	Marc Johnson's Bass Desires	ECM
Getting There	John Abercrombie	ECM
Guamba	Gary Peacock	ECM
Now You Know	Makoto Ozone	CBS
Short Stories	Bob Berg	Denon
Cross Currents	Eliane Elias	Denon
Trio	Warren Bernhardt	DMP
Incredible Journey	Bob Mintzer Big Band	DMP
Hands On	Warren Bernhardt	DMP
Camouflage	Bob Mintzer Big Band	DMP
Spectrum	Bob Mintzer Big Band	DMP
Heat Of The Moment	Warren Bernhardt	DMP
Urban Contours	Bob Mintzer Big Band	DMP
Facets	Doc Severinsen	Amherst
Time In Place	Mike Stern	Atlantic
John Patitucci	John Patitucci	GRP
Times Like These	Gary Burton	GRP
Don't Try This At Home	Michael Brecker	Impulse
So Far, So Close	Eliane Elias	Blue Note
Motion Poet	Peter Erskine	Denon
Aurora	Aurora	Denon
John Abercrombie, Marc Johnson Peter Erskine	(same)	ECM
Jigsaw	Mike Stern	Atlantic
Reunion	Gary Burton/Pat Metheny	GRP

DCI Video "Everything Is Timekeeping" with John Abercrombie & Marc Johnson